AS WE SAW IT

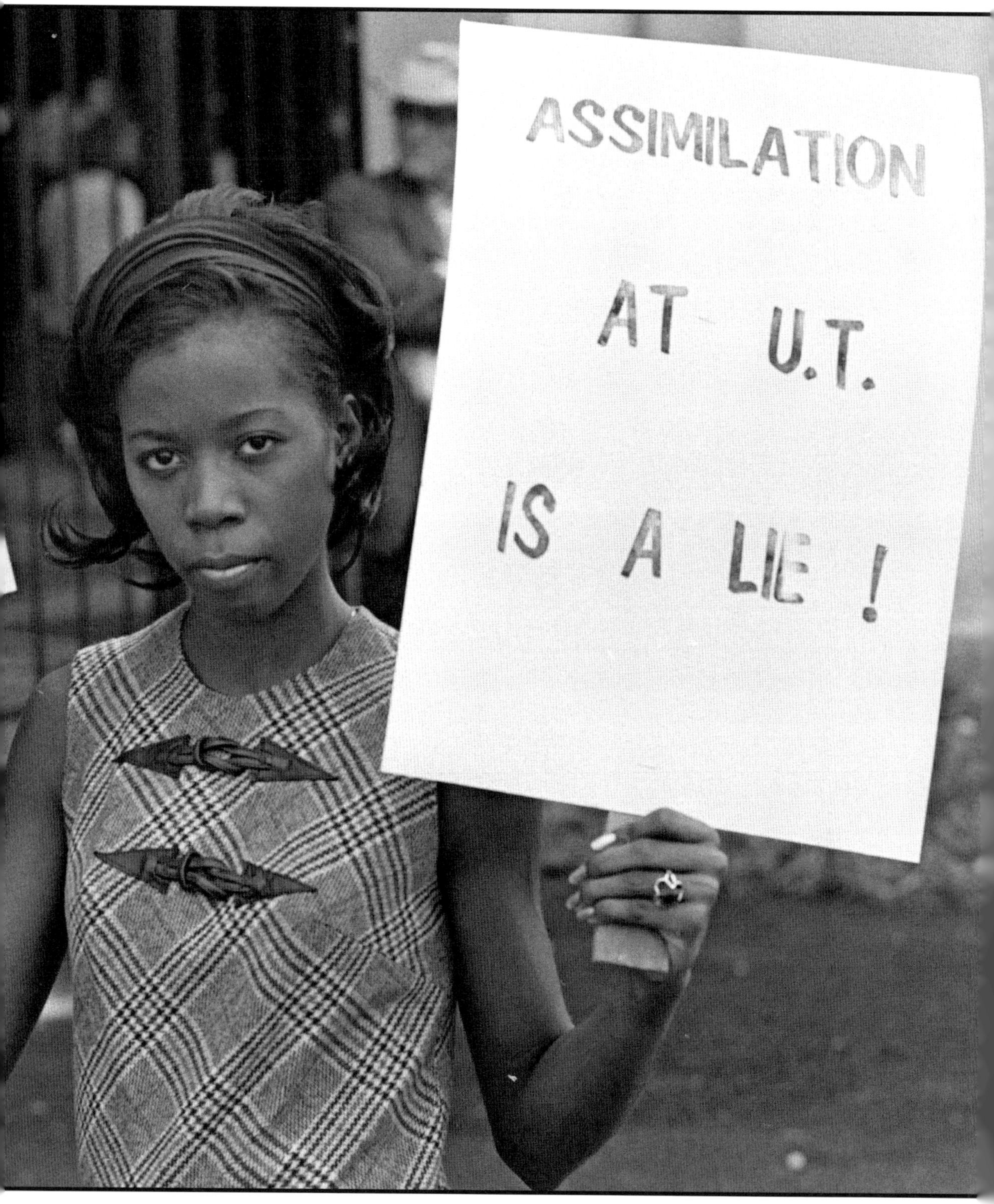
ASSIMILATION
AT U.T.
IS A LIE !

As We Saw It

THE STORY OF INTEGRATION AT THE UNIVERSITY OF TEXAS AT AUSTIN

■

Edited by

DR. GREGORY J. VINCENT,
VIRGINIA A. CUMBERBATCH, AND LESLIE A. BLAIR

with Preface by

DR. GREGORY J. VINCENT

Introduction by

VIRGINIA A. CUMBERBATCH

and Epilogue by

FRAN HARRIS

■

The Division of Diversity and Community Engagement
The University of Texas at Austin

Distributed by Tower Books, an Imprint of the University of Texas Press

Frontispiece: Texas Student Publications Collection

Requests for permission to reproduce material from this work should be sent to:
Permissions
University of Texas Press
P.O. Box 7819
Austin, TX 78713-7819
http://utpress.utexas.edu/index.php/rp-form

LIBRARY OF CONGRESS CATALOGING-IN-PUBLICATION DATA
Names: Vincent, Gregory J., editor. | Cumberbatch, Virginia A., editor. | Blair, Leslie, 1954– editor. | Harris, Fran, 1965– writer of supplementary textual content. | University of Texas at Austin. Division of Diversity and Community Engagement.
Title: As we saw it : the story of integration at the University of Texas at Austin / edited by Dr. Gregory J. Vincent, Virginia A. Cumberbatch, and Leslie A. Blair; with preface by Dr. Gregory J. Vincent, introduction by Virginia A. Cumberbatch, and epilogue by Fran Harris.
Description: First edition. | Austin : Tower Books, an imprint of the University of Texas Press, 2018. | "The Division of Diversity and Community Engagement, The University of Texas at Austin." | Includes bibliographical references and index.
Identifiers: LCCN 2017047733
    ISBN 978-1-4773-1441-8 (cloth : alk. paper)
Subjects: LCSH: University of Texas at Austin. | College integration—Texas—Austin—History. | African Americans—Education (Higher)—Texas—History. | Blacks—Education (Higher)—Texas—History.
Classification: LCC LC214.23.A97 A7 2018 | DDC 378.764/31—dc23
LC record available at https://lccn.loc.gov/2017047733

CONTENTS

ACKNOWLEDGEMENTS

LIKE THE STORY DOCUMENTED in the following pages, it takes the contributions of an entire community to complete the narrative. As such, we would like to extend our gratitude and appreciation to the following people and organizations for their support and inspired work to make *As We Saw It* a reality:

The *Alcalde*
Almetris "Mama" Duren
Alison Beck, Dolph Briscoe Center for American History
Dolph Briscoe Center for American History
Dr. Aileen Bumphus
Louise Iscoe
The Precursors, Inc.
The University of Texas Athletics

Special thanks go to DDCE art director Ron Bowdoin for his conception and guidance for the book cover. We would also like to extend our gratitude to others who contributed to the book by providing background information, written stories, or photographs:

Fred Alexander
Doris Askew-Hicks
Kevin Almasy
Dorothy Cato
Amy Crossette
Maudie Ates Fogle
Meg Halpin
Col. Leon Holland
Peggy Holland
Louise Iscoe

Christopher Palmer
Sherry Reddick
Jessica Sinn
Anitha Mitchell
Sheryl Griffin Bozeman

And many thanks to those who allowed us to interview them for stories:

Hoover Alexander
Jody Conradt
Exalton Delco
DeLoss Dodds
Dr. Edwin Dorn
Mamie Hans Ewing
Rodney Griffin
Walter "Chris" Jones
Roosevelt Leaks
Bill Lyons
Emmanuel McKinney
Judge Harriet Murphy
John Robinson
Retha Swindell
Bettye Taylor

Several of those who submitted stories or were interviewed for this publication are no longer with us including John Chase, Norcell Haywood, W. Astor Kirk, and Beulah Taylor. It is our intention that the stories here honor their memory for years to come.

PREFACE

To the Precursors, our first Black students
at the University of Texas, thank you.

THANK YOU FOR HOLDING YOURSELVES to the highest of standards. Thank you for choosing love over hate, perseverance over apathy, and unity over discord. Thank you for transforming our university, preserving your history, staying close with one another, and refusing to forget. Because of you, when our Black alumni return to campus, they can feel at home.

The Precursors, the generation of fearless Black students who desegregated the University of Texas at Austin and whose stories are recounted in the pages of this book, are responsible for both reconciling our past and providing reason to have spaces for cultural recognition today. It began nearly seventy years ago when a postal worker from Houston dreamed of entering law school. Though it would take more time than it should have, the University of Texas at Austin became the first major research institution in the South to desegregate following the abolishment of "separate but equal." Change began in 1950 with the Supreme Court decision in the landmark *Sweatt v. Painter* case. The Supreme Court ruling allowed Heman Marion Sweatt to enroll at the University of Texas School of Law and other Blacks to enroll in graduate school. Not until 1956 were undergraduates allowed to enroll, paving the way for our students today. Yet many stories of our first students have not been told.

So much of the racial progress we have made on this campus has been dependent on not forgetting. On this foundation we have created new departments, such as African and African Diaspora Studies and the Department of Mexican American and Latina/o Studies, hired diverse faculty and staff, founded and funded student and campus organizations such as the Multicultural Engagement Center, and increased our alumni outreach.

When the Precursors first stepped foot on campus, they entered an aca-

Dr. Gregory J. Vincent, then vice president of UT's Division of Diversity and Community Engagement (far left) stands with the 29th president of UT-Austin and members of the first black undergraduate class to enter in 1956, during the celebration of the landmark event in 2016. (From left to right) Dr. Gregory J. Vincent; Lola Hawkins-Ford; Willie Cleveland Jordan Jr.; Col. Leon Holland; Agnes Hill-Knight; Eva Goins-Simmons; June Frances Simpson-McCoy; Walker Eugene Hunt; Norma Jean Hancock-Lawrence; Charles Murray Miles; Edna Odessa Humphries-Rhambo; Gregory Fenves, UT-Austin president; William H. McRaven, University of Texas System chancellor. (Photo by Brian Birzer)

demic space that was openly hostile to their existence. Though united in their struggle, life was not easy. For almost all, they were the lone African American in their classes, and many would go the entire day without seeing a face that looked like theirs. In 1971, a decade and a half after the university was desegregated, African Americans represented less than 1 percent of the student population. Heman Sweatt's nephew, also named Heman Sweatt, tells of arriving on campus in the early 1970s and not seeing another Black student for nearly two weeks.

Although some of UT's first Black students matriculated with few challenges, many of the earliest of the Precursors experienced opposition and resistance to their presence on campus. Black students were excluded from campus life on an institution-mandated basis, banned from joining the athletic teams or participating in any on-campus social clubs or activities. With few options for room and board, most of the first Black students were forced to live off campus, commute from the all-Black Samuel Huston College or Tillotson College (now Huston-Tillotson University), or if one could obtain a residence, make do with the unsightly, unequal, and un-air-conditioned accommodations in the San Jacinto barracks, Whitis Co-op, or Bracken-ridge. To make ends meet usually meant holding down multiple jobs—if they could be found. As if that weren't enough, our earliest Precursors inhabited a campus at a time before much of the nation's civil rights legislation.

The accolades tied to the Precursors—bold, daring, courageous—cannot be overstated. It is difficult to put words to their experience because it was not one that my generation could ever imagine having to inhabit. I was fortunate, having grown up in a spiritual community that fostered unconditional love, where, because of men and women like the Precursors, I was enabled to pursue the heights of academia, law, and civic leadership.

Yes, the Precursors were fearless, but they were so much more than that. They are and forever will be central to the story of the University of Texas, the city of Austin, the state of Texas, and higher education across the nation. Because of the example these men and women set, and the blueprint they laid for all, we have had the opportunity to become educators, politicians, business owners, lawyers, and judges. Their social activism, peacefully demonstrated, and their persistence to take what was rightfully theirs—a best in class education—made all that I've accomplished possible.

This book is an acknowledgment that although the integration of the University of Texas was far from perfect, we must never forget our history and the stories of those who changed our arc forever. This process of integration, scars and all, will be recognized and remembered and used as inspiration to carry out the ongoing work of diversity and inclusion that remains vital to our university and our nation.

I thank Louise Iscoe and the late Almetris "Mama" Duren for authoring what in many ways was the first edition of this book, *Overcoming: A History of Black Integration at the University of Texas at Austin*. Published in 1979, the book covers the first two decades of integration at UT—a unique period in the life of a large state university as Duren and Iscoe explained it. I also thank Louise Iscoe for the vital role she played in researching and collecting many of the stories in this collection. Likewise, I thank Virginia Cumberbatch, who served as lead researcher, writer, and photo editor for this manuscript, for dedicating her time as a graduate student in our division to this important effort. Without her dedication, this material may have remained an online resource only.

It is important that we recognize that these stories also have contemporary meaning. As we have seen in the case of *Fisher v. University of Texas*, there is still much to be done both on our campus and in society to increase cultural understanding and inclusion.

We are overjoyed to share the stories that document the integration of the University of Texas at Austin through the eyes of the Precursors. To quote

Louise Iscoe and Mama Duren, "Progress is relative, and the knowledge that people draw from history is based in large part on the background that they bring to it."[1]

We hope that you enjoy our history, "as they saw it."

—DR. GREGORY J. VINCENT

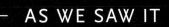

AS WE SAW IT

INTRODUCTION

THE HISTORICAL NARRATIVES we choose to recognize, document, and curate often shape institutional memory and set a precedent for an institution's values and priorities. Such is true for institutions of higher learning. The monuments built on campus, the plaques that adorn hallways, and the stately names that are inscribed on the sides of buildings are representative of the stories we wish to acknowledge and account. Without documentation, individual experiences and institutional knowledge are lost, and consequently the breadth of cultural processes and contributions is abbreviated or, in some cases, eradicated from public purview. *As We Saw It: The Story of Integration at the University of Texas at Austin* seeks to document the stories of those individuals who pioneered the way for today's continued conversations of race, diversity, and inclusion. *As We Saw It* is a representative sample of the common experiences, unique trials, and unprecedented triumphs of UT Austin's first generation of Black students from 1951 through 1975.

One of the most powerful drivers of how race is described, citizenship is defined, and politics of access are determined is quite simple: the words we use, the stories we choose to tell, and the methodology we use to document such narratives. As America and the world engage in ongoing conversations on civil rights and renegotiate institutional and political practices of equality and access, how we frame experiences and elevate historically marginalized stories in the context of education is critical. In America's twenty-first century, we've been forced to grapple with the social context that ignited Black Lives Matter, Islamophobia, and Mexican and immigrant civil rights. As Longhorns we've been asked to come to terms with policy and practice that would foster the conversation surrounding *Fisher v. UT* and the relocation of the Jefferson Davis statue from the main mall of campus.

So how do we use storytelling as a tool to cultivate an environment where our diverse student populations feel heard, feel included, and, most important, can see themselves? We all know that the historical narrative of America, and its understanding of race, has been fundamentally contorted to empower white America; therefore, generations of young people of color have

Overcoming: A History of Black Integration at the University of Texas at Austin

ALMETRIS MARSH DUREN
in association with LOUISE ISCOE

Overcoming: A History of Black Integration at the University of Texas served as a foundational piece to *As We Saw It*. Louise Iscoe and Mama Duren's dedication to collecting and documenting these stories is unparalleled.

been silenced—their stories being told for them, influencing and in some cases completely undermining their educational experience and opportunities to thrive socially and academically. Good storytelling has the power to reconcile some of these historic and systemic tragedies. In 2010, the Division of Diversity and Community Engagement (DDCE) approached Louise Iscoe, coauthor of *Overcoming: A History of Black Integration at the University of Texas*, to help document the story of the first Black students to step foot on and survive the Forty Acres from 1951 to 1975. Iscoe and Almetris "Mama" Duren, the first Black dorm mother at UT Austin, compiled the *Overcoming* book based on Duren's experiences and her collection of photos and news clippings about the Black experience at UT. Other than two books written by Dwonna Goldstone and Gary Lavergne on the history of integration at UT Austin and the Heman Sweatt case, Duren and Iscoe's twenty-five-page hardback in some ways serves as our only comprehensive record of the Black experience at UT Austin.[1]

The integration of the University of Texas at Austin is a story that transcends the Forty Acres, Austin, and Texas education. The *Sweatt* decision, in fact, set the stage for *Brown v. Board of Education of Topeka*, which desegregated schools nationwide. That case and the UT Austin experience, which now includes two other prominent legal cases in *Hopwood v. Texas* and *Fisher v. University of Texas*, continue to drive national conversations on race, inclusion, and diversity in higher education.

At the Twenty-Fourth Annual Heman Sweatt Symposium on Civil Rights in 2010, for the first time, a group of the earliest Black students at UT, known as the Precursors, participated in a panel discussion, sharing their stories of what the UT Austin campus was like in the 1950s. For some of these participants, it was their first visit to campus since their college days. It was clear to staff of the DDCE that these stories and the legacy of this particular group of alumni were critical to moving diversity, inclusion, and equality efforts forward at the university. Likewise, in telling their stories, UT's Black alumni felt heard, appreciated, and remembered, an experience contrary to their time on campus as students.

Shortly thereafter, the DDCE began working on a project to collect stories from the alumni and work toward their publication online and ultimately in this book. A few of the stories of those first Black students were fairly well known. Stories of Heman Sweatt, the first Black student to enroll in the Law School; John Chase, the first Black student to enroll in the School of Architecture; and Barbara Smith Conrad, the woman who broke color barriers in the UT Department of Theatre and Dance and went on to become a world-renown opera singer, were generally known, as were athletic standouts like Heisman Trophy winner Earl Campbell. Their stories were the ones strongly touted in collateral material, well documented in the university's archives, and often covered in *Daily Texan* newspaper stories. While the contributions of these students were groundbreaking and critical to the UT narrative, they cannot solely represent the full experience of integrating the Forty Acres.

Members of the first class of Black undergraduate students celebrate the sixtieth anniversary of their admittance in 1956. For many present, it was the first time back on campus since graduating. (From left to right) Jerry Ann Cannon-Hunter; Eva Goins-Simmons; Earnestyne Yvonne Bell-Terry; Lola Hawkins-Ford; Agnes Hill-Knight; Edna Odessa Humphries-Rhambo; Charles Murray Miles; Willie Cleveland Jordan Jr.; Walker Eugene Hunt; June Frances Simpson-McCoy; Mamie Hans-Ewing; Col. Leon Holland; Norma Jean Hancock-Lawrence; David Washington. (Photo by Brian Birzer)

In 2013 precursors gathered for the annual Heman Sweatt Symposium, which serves to honor the legacy of Heman Sweatt and those who continue the work of social advocacy. (From left to right) William "Bill" Spearman; Lonnie Fogle; Maudie Ates-Fogle; Freddie "Fred" Alexander; Judith Jenkins; Dr. Gregory Vincent; Judge Harriet Murphy; Jacquelyn Hawkins; Peggy Drake Holland; Col. Leon Holland. (Photo by Shelton Lewis)

Although we are indebted to the support and resources of the Dolph Briscoe Center for American History, we found that even a center that focuses on recovering and curating American history lacked comprehensive records.[2] On our first visits to the center, where we worked with librarians to identify the best sources to contextualize the story of the university's integration, we were handed a folder that simply read "Negros at UT"; inside it rested looseleaf papers and photos, most of which had been donated by Mama Duren, lacking time stamps or record of who was captured in the photos. Furthermore, we were hard pressed to find school records that provided a definitive list of all the Black students who entered UT in 1956, when undergraduate enrollment was officially integrated. No comprehensive record was preserved of the estimated one hundred Black students who entered UT that year. It is difficult to grapple with the logic that after nearly a century of thwarting the coloring of the Forty Acres, no effort had been made to list, track, document, or remember the Black pioneers of 1956, then or since then.

Several years earlier, Colonel Leon Holland, who was a freshman in 1956, had painstakingly begun a months-long process of identifying all Black undergraduates who enrolled that same year. But there had been discussion that there may have been students missing from that list. We wanted an accurate count and the names of the first Black undergraduates. So the process to uncover those names required the review of nearly two hundred rolls of microfilm transcripts, categorized by alphabetized surnames, not class year. The 112 Black students of 1956 were thus identified or confirmed by searching for students with a known Black segregated high school listed on their transcript.

This process didn't discourage us; it merely reinforced the need for *As We Saw It* to exist, and, more important, it increased the urgency to reach out to the Precursors and document their stories. Whether they submitted their narrative or we sat down with them for a cup of coffee in their living rooms, recounting their memorable, painful, and sometimes ignored experiences before, during, or after time on campus, their stories would be told. DDCE began a "Share Your Story" campaign, encouraging Black alum from 1951 to 1975 to either submit their firsthand account of their time at UT or to arrange a time to meet with DDCE staff or affiliates. The "Share Your Story" campaign resulted in more than thirty stories documented. We would use these stories to cement their time and contributions to UT's social and cultural landscape and to educate, empower, and elevate the current experience of students of color. The students of the twenty-first century needed to know that there were footprints etched before their arrival, that they were ever connected and ever indebted to these men and women. The uncanny relevancy to the challenges to democracy, diversity, and racism of today set the tone and expectation for this book's context and structure. We have sought to organize the book in a way that thematically ties shared experiences, outlining the mirrored experience of the Precursors with that of students today: from dorm life and the role of athletes as de facto activists to the intersection of womanhood and race and the impact of city and federal policy on students' experiences on campus. The epilogue, written by UT alumna Fran Harris, who entered UT in 1981, connects her generation to the current discussion of diversity, inclusion, and place on college campuses.

This book is meant to provide insight into a generally underdocumented part of UT's historical lexicon and honor the contributions of Black students to the cultural, social, and political landscape of the Forty Acres, past and present. The material in this book was collected primarily through first-person interviews and accounts, contextualized through archival research. Thus, the focus and tone of the book reflect those of collective memory and personal reflection amid the backdrop of revolutionary legislation. John Woods once said, "Many people who have weathered the earliest years of integration have changed their views over time. Many look back in disbelief at what were accepted practices in those days and are astounded at how so much progress in thought as well as action has taken place in a 30-year span. Others, particularly younger persons who did not live through the trying times of the first steps toward integration, don't focus on the progress that has been made, but only what still remains to be done."[3] This collection of stories, however, does not attempt to represent a comprehensive report of the politics, procedures, or policies surrounding the integration of UT or convince anyone that the process of integration and racial equity has been reached at UT or at any institution of higher learning. This is the story of integration at a predominantly white university, through the eyes of those who pioneered and persevered.

The story of integration at UT amid the backdrop of the Jim Crow South is complex and momentous—a story that necessitates understanding and sharing. *As We Saw It* is a representative sample of important narratives that helped create and continues to shape both the infrastructure and conversations of inclusion, equality, and access in higher education. The university's commitment to its holistic admissions process in the *Fisher v. University of Texas* lawsuit is an example of how UT Austin has helped drive the conversation. Although focused on the future of equality, equity, and access, we cannot forget the past, as it plays a vital role informing the future. These alum should be remembered and honored as we continue to strive for richly diverse and inclusive campuses across the country. What is outlined in the following pages reconciles past grievances toward the university around segregation and racialized policies, while serving as a catalyst to inform discourse around the continued isolation that students of color currently experience on the Forty Acres.

The University of Texas at Austin campus in 1921. (The Dolph Briscoe Center for American History)

CHAPTER ONE

New Beginnings in Texas Education

WHILE THE MOMENT COMMONLY DISCUSSED, celebrated, and cited as the turning point for both the University of Texas at Austin and predominantly white institutions across the state of Texas is the *Sweatt v. Painter* lawsuit and Heman Marion Sweatt's admittance to the UT Law School, the colorization of the Forty Acres was a process, the result of numerous courageous efforts throughout the years. In 1885, only two years after the university opened its doors, an African American man (whose name goes undocumented) applied for admission to UT but was denied access. The basis for his rejection was officially listed as "the admittance of negroes is not of standard practice."[1] Although it would be more than forty years before another formal attempt was made, Texas institutions would have continued pressure to offer pathways to education for Black students. Most Black students who attempted to attend predominantly white institutions, whether private or public, were met with regulatory and social roadblocks.

The second attempt to integrate the University of Texas at Austin came in October 1938, when the NAACP hoped to force the legislature to provide scholarships for Black Texans to attend institutions of higher education out of state. George L. Allen "had only applied to UT in order to be refused admission." In a 1982 interview he said, "The only wrench in the whole machine was that they admitted me."[2] He arrived on campus to attend a business psychology and salesmanship class. His mere presence confounded the other students and administrators.[3] No such defiance or challenge to the unwritten yet enacted regulations of racial discriminatory policy of the school had ever taken place, but to the disbelief of Allen, UT allowed him to take the class, completely thwarting Allen and the NAACP's plan to use the opportunity to sue the state.

A few days later, however, Professor C. P. Brewer arranged to meet with Allen to notify him the school was asking him to withdraw from the class. After Allen refused, his registration was cancelled and he was prohibited from attending class. He and the NAACP threatened to sue. In response to the threat, an out-of-state scholarship program was established by the state legislature in 1939. Moving forward, the State of Texas agreed to pay the tuition of any African American who wished to acquire a degree beyond a bachelor's degree at an out-of-state school that admitted Negroes. For nearly a decade, the State of Texas and several other Southern states, including Maryland and Virginia, avoided admitting students of color by offering state dollars to fund their academic pursuits in other states. The state, rather than radicalize policy and deconstruct discriminatory practices, sent Black students to schools, primarily in the West and Northeast, on the dime of the State of Texas.[4] It would take a formal change in legislation to redefine state higher education. Ironically, the state-supported payment to send students to other states for their education was effectively outlawed by the Supreme Court in December 1938 in *Missouri ex rel. Gaines v. Canada*—about six months before state legislators passed the Texas bill.

Though the NAACP had desired its implementation, the scholarship plan did not satisfy the ideals or educational pursuits of many. Black families noted the program did not address severe discrepancies in the quality of secondary and higher education serving the Black population in Texas. "I don't mean this in a negative way, but Huston-Tillotson was just not an adequate substitute for the University of Texas," an alumnus stated. "My parents wanted us to have the opportunity to attend the school for which we were best qualified, and that was UT."[5] This sentiment was shared by many African Americans throughout the state who wished to pursue advanced degrees. Some Black Texans voiced displeasure at sending students away from their families and communities. Many saw it as an intermediate goal in the fight to get Black students admitted to the University of Texas. But the University of Texas had made quite clear its plans to resist such progressive action. UT Austin regent Orville Bullington stated in a letter in January 1944, "There is not the slightest danger of any Negro attending the University of Texas, regardless of what Franklin D[.], Eleanor, or the Supreme Court says, so long as you have a Board of Regents with as much intestinal fortitude as the present one has."[6] The system was surely flawed; by the end of 1939, only 53 students out of the 180 who had applied for the out-of-state scholarship program had received assistance, leaving more than half of the twenty-five thousand dollars allocated for such tuition payments in state coffers.[7] Furthermore, it depleted the Black Texas community of the social and political benefits, expertise, and thought leadership of those educated residents sent out of state.

After World War II, the NAACP began to get serious about integrating the University of Texas at Austin. President Franklin Roosevelt had signed the GI Bill (formally, the Servicemen's Readjustment Act of 1944) into law, precipitating a rush on colleges and universities after the war. UT historian Joe Frantz, who was first hired at UT Austin in 1946 as a teaching as-

Young Black Austin residents protest the separate-but-equal state laws on the UT campus in the 1940s. (The Dolph Briscoe Center for American History)

sistant, wrote, "The mob of ex-servicemen arrived as expected. Enrollment jumped from its previous high of 11,000 to 17,000."[8] Not among them were Black veterans. Unsurprisingly, many veterans from the South moved to the North and West where they were being admitted to colleges and universities at high rates.[9] At the same time historically Black colleges and universities (HBCUs) in the South were forced to turn students away due to swelling enrollment and limited budgets. Very little had changed within the higher education landscape in Texas other than the legislature renaming Prairie View State Normal and Industrial College to "Prairie View University," despite providing no new funding. Legislators feared Blacks would begin to apply to the state's largest university, and many knew that HB 255, the law providing scholarships to Black students to attend out-of-state colleges and universities, would not stand up to legal scrutiny. Not insignificantly, the NAACP was near its peak in membership and fund-raising potential. It was with this political climate in mind that the NAACP decided it was time to target the UT Law School and work toward its integration.[10]

The Law School at UT Austin was selected for a number of reasons. Students at UT were seen as increasingly liberal and generally favoring integration; and there were white, relatively liberal faculty members who could quiet potential tensions. The Law School had very few female students, so the concern about intermarriage likely would not be invoked. The state's oil money, which enriched the permanent university fund, was a factor as well. According to Gary Lavergne, "With the breathtaking state-owned resources Texas had at its disposal, if it could not afford to pay for separate equality for its African American population, no other segregated state could either."[11]

Finding an applicant who was courageous, dependable, and with indisputable admission credentials turned out to be difficult for the NAACP. The leadership nearly gave up and questioned whether they should pursue a lawsuit in a public school system instead, when Heman Sweatt volunteered in late October 1945. As Lavergne reminds us, Sweatt, a mail carrier at the time, "was integral to NAACP's master plan aimed at breaking down segregation in education." He also says that now, more than sixty years later, Sweatt still matters; Sweatt's case continues to guide us.[12]

■ HEMAN SWEATT

Behind Heman Marion Sweatt's slight stature and meek demeanor stood a strong and determined lineage that revered and utilized education as an avenue for political engagement, social progress, and self-enlightenment, the genetic fortitude and a social preparation that the position of "first" would demand. His family began, as far as is known, with Richard Sweatt, a slave. But author and historian Gary Lavergne considered James Leonard Sweatt Sr. the key to the family's educational and professional success. Papa Sweatt, as he was called, was highly respected by his community. Heman often shared that his father was quite a historian, and he taught him the subject at the table. "He was very sensitive and informed on the issues." According to Lavergne, when Heman was asked who were the greatest influences in his life, he said, "Number one, Papa Sweatt, and number two, Melvin Tolson, a teacher at Wiley College. According to Heman Sweatt's daughter, Dr. Hemella Sweatt, "nothing was more important to him than education. Whatever comes in second was so far distant that it didn't really matter."[13]

Heman's great-great-grandfather was one of ten graduates of Prairie View A&M's class of 1890, a class trained to become teachers for Negro schools throughout the state of Texas. James Sr. had six children, and he encouraged all of them to attend college. Decades of Sweatts produced doctors, bank executives, and educators. Born in Houston in 1912, Heman grew up in Houston's Third Ward and eventually made his way to Wiley College, an HBCU in Marshall, Texas. In 1945 Sweatt attended a meeting at which the NAACP was soliciting students to serve as a plaintiff in a law school desegregation case. The person selected had to be qualified academically to attend the school and have the determination to see the case through to its conclusion. In addition, that person would have both his or her name and life inter-twined with years of bitter litigation for civil rights in the South. He or she needed to be intelligent, courageous, and reliable.[14]

Sweatt had been preparing for this moment most of his life. After grad-uating from Wiley College in 1934, he attended the University of Michigan with hopes of pursuing medicine, but he eventually returned to Texas and began work as a postal carrier. Although education had afforded him the lux-ury of access and social clout, he was not shielded from the injustices of the Jim Crow era. During the early 1940s he participated in voter-registration drives and raised funds for lawsuits against the whites-only primary system in Texas. Likewise, Sweatt had an opportunity to write several columns for the *Houston Informer*, covering legal issues and discriminatory practices tak-ing place throughout the state. One particular issue hit close to home. Post offices had stopped promoting Blacks to supervisory positions by systemat-ically excluding them from clerical positions that would make them eligi-ble to be promoted. Being a local secretary of the National Alliance of Postal Employees, Sweatt challenged these practices. While preparing documen-tation for this case with an attorney, his admiration and interest in the law were cultivated.[15]

Sweatt began to investigate opportunities to attend law school. With the help of civil rights activist and attorney William Durham, Sweatt ac-tively pursued the only law school with the reputation to support his thirst of knowledge, the University of Texas Law School. So Sweatt raised his hand and answered the call of the NAACP to represent the organization and thou-sands of his Black peers in challenging the policies and procedures of the uni-versity. On February 26, 1946, Heman Marion Sweatt applied to the Univer-sity of Texas Law School. He met the academic requirements: a bachelor of arts from Wiley College in 1934 and twelve semester hours of graduate work at the University of Michigan in 1937. Although he was qualified academi-cally, he was denied admission due to the persistent racialized admission pol-icy. UT's rejection of Sweatt's application provided the NAACP the oppor-tunity it had been seeking, a motive to pursue legal action. The impact of Sweatt's denied access to a state school would prove to be a revolutionary act in policy, higher education, civil rights, and Texas history.

On May 26, 1946, in the State of Texas 126th District Court, Heman Mar-ion Sweatt filed a suit citing that denying him admission was an infringe-ment of his rights under the Fourteenth Amendment of the US Constitution. The court determined that if the university would establish a separate-but-equal institution for Sweatt, it would throw out the case. A year later UT opened a facility on E. Thirteenth St. near the Capitol in a basement, to be called the School of Law of the State University for Negroes. It had a couple

Heman Marion Sweatt (3rd from left) discusses the impending lawsuit with members of the NAACP legal team. (The Dolph Briscoe Center for American History)

of rooms, one or two faculty members, and no other students. The administration notified Heman Sweatt, but he refused to report for classes or attend. Instead, with the backing of the NAACP, he took his case through the courts and ultimately to the US Supreme Court.

In 1950, the Supreme Court decided in his favor, stating that the educational opportunities offered to white and Black law students by the State of Texas were not substantially equal and that the equal protection clause of the Fourteenth Amendment required that the relator (Sweatt) be admitted to the University of Texas Law School. Thus began the case that, in time, did away with the separate-but-equal rule and led to the end of segregation in the nation's public schools. On the eve of the Supreme Court decision, Sweatt's personal triumph was reaffirmed as a social victory. Thurgood Marshall called to congratulate him, shouting, "We won the big one!" That week Sweatt also received a letter from Marshall stating, "You are entitled to the fullest credit for a job well done. If it had not been for your courage and refusal to be swayed by others, this victory would not have been possible."[16]

Sweatt and George Washington Jr. were among the first six Blacks to enter the UT Law School in the fall of 1950. Washington had aspired to become a lawyer most of his life but had wavered in his confidence that he would be afforded the opportunity. Although fully aware of the precarious circumstances and immense pressure that he and Sweatt would face as they pursued their degrees, he resolved such fears quietly and expediently. His wife reflected on the moment, sharing that his only concern "was doing well in school and getting a law degree." For both men to succeed, the emotions inherent in breaking ground and forging trails would need to become secondary to the task at hand, graduating. Washington, with the support of

family and perhaps because he had avoided the stresses of the trial, graduated. Sweatt, however, did not. He entered UT Law School in 1950, then dropped out after two years because of a combination of factors that included poor health, subpar grades, and family strains, all problems exacerbated by the stress of his long fight through the courts.[17]

Following Sweatt's historical win in 1950, UT opened its graduate courses to all qualified Black graduate students. With that decision, UT became the first institution of higher education in the South required by law to admit Blacks to its graduate programs. In countless interviews, Sweatt's family has pointed out that their family mantra, "education, persistence, discipline, civility," created the strength that enabled Heman Sweatt to withstand the difficulties

Sweatt stands in line at Gregory Gym to register for classes in 1950. (The Dolph Briscoe Center for American History)

he faced in serving as plaintiff in this historic case. "He hardly ever spoke about the case. And if he did, it was more of a factual conversation, maybe just reciting what happened, some of the facts of the case, not really the emotional side," recalled Hemella Sweatt. Heman Sweatt's nephew, also named Heman Sweatt, remembers his uncle telling him some of the experiences that he went through. "In the late forties, while trying to enter law school, he was asked to come to a meeting one evening at the Driskill Hotel in Austin. So he said he went to the hotel, he went up to the suite, and there he saw a room full of men, and on the table, twenty-seven thousand dollars cash sitting there. And the men told him, 'This is yours; you can have all of it; just take it and go away.' He easily could have scooped up the money—a pretty nice amount today, so you can imagine what it was equal to in the forties—but he just turned his back and walked out of the room."[18] Sweatt's conviction to

Sweatt studying in the early 1950s. (The Dolph Briscoe Center for American History)

take part in the academic fortune of the ivory tower of Texas outweighed any monetary settlement.

Sweatt endured many threats to his life, often leaving him vulnerable and trapped. According to his nephew Heman Sweatt, "He once shared that one day after class he was afraid to leave the building. If it had not been for the law students gathering around him and escorting him out, he really believed that there would have been some tragic ending, and he was very grateful to his white counterparts in law school for coming to his aid."[19] This consistent physical and psychological warfare was indicative of the experience of many of the first Black students: confronted with both the threat to one's existence on campus and the pressures to wage a way forward for other Black students. As Dr. William Sweatt observed during the Twenty-Fifth Annual Heman Sweatt Symposium,

We're reserved people, we're serious people, and we keep things to ourselves a lot of times. That's good in certain situations, such as being the plaintiff in this case. We're taught your word is your bond. So if you're in a pressure situation, you know you're going to stick to it no matter what the pressure is. But on the other side, it affects you because you try to be this pillar of strength, but when you're here at the university and people are throwing rocks at you and burning your house, you know that's got to affect you emotionally. There are certain people, like Heman, who will hold it in . . . but it takes a toll on you inside, it takes a toll on you physically. I think that's what he dealt with.[20]

Gary Lavergne poignantly defines the characteristic that allows for such pursuit despite incredible roadblocks. "The one valuable lesson that this man could teach us all is civility. If you want a lesson in civility, then you study the life of Heman Marion Sweatt. In five years of research, I never encountered a single moment where this man returned hatred with more hatred. I could not uncover a single quote where he denigrated anyone, even the most vile racist who threatened him, or the State of Texas, or the University of Texas. This was a very gracious man."[21]

Not long after Sweatt dropped out of law school, Whitney M. Young (who at the time was serving as the National Urban League's chief executive officer) offered him a full scholarship to enter a master's degree program in social work at Atlanta University, where he earned the degree and later accepted a position with the Urban League in Cleveland. Eight years later he relocated to the Atlanta office. In Atlanta he remarried, and there his daughter Hemella was born. Lavergne once said of Sweatt, "He faced a lot at one time while he was here, but nobody chased him away. When he wanted to leave, he left on his own, and he left with his dignity."[22] Such dignity was and is Heman Sweatt's legacy.

■ W. ASTOR KIRK

The connection between Austin's oldest standing institution of higher learning, Huston-Tillotson University (HT), and the University of Texas at Austin is no more apparent than through the life and activism of W. Astor Kirk. Having carved out his place in Austin's political sphere, Kirk, a political science professor at HT, became well known for his community work on civil rights and racial justice. Having served on the faculty at Tillotson College for some time,[23] Astor Kirk wanted to deepen his academic portfolio and expand his knowledge in government to better serve his students.

On December 4, 1947, Kirk applied to the graduate school of the University of Texas at Austin to pursue a PhD in government. Although his application was rejected, Kirk strongly believed that Texas had a legal duty to provide an opportunity for him to further his education. It had provided such an opportunity for whites, and under the 1896 separate-but-equal rule of *Plessy v. Ferguson*, he and all Black students were entitled to equal treatment.

"That year I came to the firm conclusion that it would be virtually impossible for me to realize my vision of a successful and responsible college teaching career without an earned doctorate in political science. That was the sole motivation behind my application for admission to the UT graduate school. I was not attempting to further the NAACP's civil rights strategy in Texas, but only taking a necessary step to prepare myself for a career as a college professor at Huston-Tillotson," Kirk explained.[24] Kirk's application was ul-

Members of a Huston-Tillotson College class in the late 1940s. At the time the school was
Tillotson College, where Astor Kirk taught government. The school predated the University
of Texas at Austin and not only was responsible for educating many of the future leaders
of the city and state but also provided a space for teachers and other professionals to work
and nurture their scholarship. (The Dolph Briscoe Center for American History)

timately denied because, according to Max Ficthenbaum, assistant registrar
at the time, state law prohibited Blacks from enrolling in the UT graduate
school. The *Austin American-Statesman* documented the circumstances:

> Astor Kirk made application for graduate work to Max Fichtenbaum,
> assistant registrar, but his application was denied as "one being not le-
> gal." The nattily-dressed assistant professor of political science at Til-
> lotson said that he would take other action to gain admission to the
> University "but I have not decided as yet what course of action that
> will be." Fichtenbaum told Kirk that he was at the wrong place, and
> that he should apply at Texas State University at Houston for Negroes.
> "I did that," Kirk replied in a calm, even voice, "and I have letters here
> from both the registrar and president of that institution informing me
> that they do not offer the course of study I desire." Fichtenbaum went

on to say that "we are prohibited by law from admitting you, . . . [according to the] laws of the Constitution and the State Legislature."[25]

On the day Kirk applied for admission, the afternoon media carried stories concerning his application and its rejection. He was deluged with calls requesting interviews and appearances at meetings to explain why he really applied to the university and what he intended to do about the university's refusal to accept his application. He declined all such requests for the time being except one, that of the UT Student Chapter of the NAACP. In 1947, a number of university students who believed the Jim Crow system of education was incompatible with fundamental democratic principles and values had taken the courageous step of organizing the student chapter. "I felt I had a moral obligation to be as responsive to and supportive of that student chapter as possible," Kirk recalled, "so I agreed to speak at a public meeting that the chapter sponsored off campus at the university YMCA." Excerpts from an article in the student newspaper explain the events that transpired at that meeting:

> W. Astor Kirk, professor of government at [Huston-]Tillotson, decried the inadequacy of present facilities available in Texas for higher education for Negroes. . . . He substantiated his argument with statistics from the United States Office of Education and the Research Bureau of Howard University. "There are glaring differences in facilities afforded for white students and those for Negro students in Texas. This is apparently true for lower education, but it is even more evident in higher education." Mr. Kirk went on to say that he wanted to further his education in Texas because he expects to remain here and must have the contacts which are so valuable in acquiring higher education.[26]

Kirk was adamant about making it clear that his primary goal was to enter a doctoral program as soon as possible, not to take on the University of Texas as an adversary. With the encouragement and support of his wife, Vivian, he had deliberately opted for a college teaching career in political science rather than a career as a lawyer. In order to respond to media inquiries and ease public tensions about his intentions and motivation as merely an academic pursuing resources rather than a political instigator, he issued a prepared press release:

> In view of the fact that the courses that I wish to take are not offered at any institution in the state now available to me, I plan to take the

necessary steps to determine the validity of the refusal of admission to
the University of Texas Graduate School. I feel that my native state of
Texas is under obligation to furnish me the course of study I desire.

Astor discussed the university's rejection of his application with Professor
James H. Morton, president of the Austin Branch of the NAACP. At their
first regular meeting in the new year, the Austin branch agreed to sponsor
his case, and the board of directors voted to request the NAACP to initiate
"appropriate legal proceedings" against the university. On April 12, 1948, the
NAACP lawyers filed a suit on Kirk's behalf in the Twelfth District Court
of the State of Texas. The university's Board of Regents and the state's attorney general realized their legal vulnerability under the Sipuel Doctrine of the
US Supreme Court. Hence, they negotiated an amendment with Texas State
University for Negroes (TSUN), which stated, "The University of Texas shall
offer graduate work for Negroes not available at Texas State University." However, it had a problematic clause: courses offered by UT "shall be operated
separately and apart from the campus of The University of Texas."

In December 1949, the board of trustees of the recently established TSUN
announced publicly its approval of the amendment of the Inter-University
Contract. To preclude possible procedural problems at the trial of Kirk's
case, the same official documents sent to the University of Texas were also
forwarded by registered special delivery US mail to the registrar of TSUN.
On January 7, 1950, Craig S. Cullinan, chairman of the board of trustees of
TSUN, announced to the press that the board had received and approved the
application pursuant to the Inter-University Contract, that the application
would be forwarded to the University of Texas, and that Kirk would start
graduate studies at the beginning of the second semester (February 1950) of
the academic year 1949–50.

The *Austin American-Statesman* carried a two-column front-page news
story on January 8, 1950, regarding Kirk's admission to UT's Graduate
School under contract. "That contract," university president T. S. Painter explained, "provides that the University will offer graduate work to Negroes
that is not yet available at the relatively new Houston school." Painter said
that Negro students admitted to the university under contract would study
on a segregated basis. "Separate classrooms would be provided," he said. On
January 30, Kirk signed up for two courses, international organization and
administration and American state administration, and paid the required
tuition fee of twenty-six dollars. Once he had signed up for the courses and
paid the registration fee, university administrators were forced to make an official decision about where the courses would be taught and to inform Kirk
who his professors would be and where he should report for classes. After

signing up for the courses, Kirk traveled home to the comfort of his home-town and peaceful cornfields of East Texas. He needed time to escape the media frenzy, spend time with his parents, and clear his head before the daunting undertaking to enter the hostile Forty Acres. He recalls reflecting on a childhood vision, when he heard God tell him, "If you accept the exist-ing circumstances of your life, then that means denying your God-given abil-ity to visualize something radically different and much better. In turn, that means rejecting all possibilities of ever achieving an alternate and more re-warding set of life circumstances."

At the beginning of February, the university officially notified Kirk that his classes would be taught off campus at the YMCA across from the cam-pus on Guadalupe Street and that he would be the only student in each class. On February 7, Kirk went to the class in international organization and ad-ministration and met with Professor Charles A. Timm of the UT Govern-ment Department. A half-dozen reporters confronted him as he entered the YMCA. Before delivering a statement, Kirk made clear to his professor his intention to take the course. "I explained my situation and assured him that I had absolutely no adverse or hard feelings toward him. He said he under-stood my position and added, 'I probably would take the same course of ac-tion if I were in your shoes.' I gave him a copy of a statement I had written and told him I would provide it to representatives of the press on my way out of the YMCA." The statement said, in part:

> I cannot accept the arrangements offered me by the University of Texas. If provisions had been made for me on the campus of the uni-versity, where I could cherish at least the feeling that I was a student there, my reaction to the whole question would be entirely different. I believe I could have accepted arrangements on the university cam-pus without establishing in the public mind that I was completely lacking in self-respect, integrity, and a sense of civic responsibility.
>
> Although I earnestly desire to further my education in my chosen profession, my conscience will not permit me to accept arrangements proffered by the University of Texas.

Kirk recollected that most of his Austin associates and friends, both Black and white, believed he had made the right decision in not accepting the off-campus, single-student classes the university offered. But more impor-tant to Kirk was the opinion of his students at Tillotson College who ex-pressed to him how proud they were of his stance. One student shared, "We are so proud of you for practicing yourself what you preach to us." His stead-fast conviction and perseverance would have a great effect on the future of

Black life at UT and in Austin. He not only fought for his right to attend UT Austin but was involved in other civil rights issues while a resident in the city.

On June 5, 1950, the US Supreme Court rendered its decision in *Sweatt v. Painter*, ordering Sweatt's admission to the University of Texas Law School on a nonsegregated basis. At that time, the Board of Regents then agreed to open the Graduate School and professional schools of the university to Blacks on an integrated basis. The new policy was to take effect with the beginning of summer school in 1950. Kirk enrolled in the UT Graduate School in September 1950. In the summer of 1958, he graduated from UT Austin with a doctorate in government, with specific concentration on public administration, administrative law, and economics. He recalled that "during the time I was a graduate student at UT, I was also a resident of Austin. Therefore, I did not encounter some of the challenging experiences of campus living that the first African American undergraduate students faced. At the same time, I continued my teaching career at Huston-Tillotson University." The flexibility to navigate from campus back to a defined community in East Austin provided a sense of security and support, a support system that he would rely on heavily as he continued his work in resisting injustice in the city.

Kirk recalled, "Initially, when I enrolled in the UT graduate school, I had a concern that my professors might manifest a negative reaction to my social-change and civil rights activities in the Greater Austin community, especially since some of the community social policies my students and I chose to challenge involved UT professors." Such apprehension and concern stemmed from his visibility and engagement in protesting Austin's discriminatory practices—activities that were commonly documented and discussed on campus.

One such incident concerned the protest of racial segregation in the use of the Austin Public Library. From 1933 to 1951 the City of Austin had provided public library services to its residents on a racially segregated basis. The Austin Public Library designated the small George Washington Carver branch in East Austin as the only library to serve African Americans. Any library materials African Americans wanted that were unavailable at Carver but were located in the central library or some other branch could be sent to Carver on special requisition. According to Kirk, "When I spoke to City Manager Walter Seaholm about this practice, he told me that there was no written policy about it. 'In this case,' he said, 'settled practice has become policy, which everybody understands.' At that moment I decided to initially protest indirectly, to 'overburden' the system."

So, Kirk went to the Carver branch and requested the Harvard Classics.

The central library wanted to know which volume. He said he was engaged in a research project and needed the whole set. Two days later he requested the *Encyclopedia of Social Sciences*. The same question was raised. He gave the same answer. His third request was for all volumes of the *World Book of Knowledge*. The Carver branch staff informed Kirk that City Librarian Mary Rice said he could use the central library for research if he would agree to stand and not use any of the seats. After receiving this information, Kirk decided the time was ripe to make a formal protest to the City Council. In July 1951 Kirk formally asked the City Council for a declaration of policy regarding "Austin residents' use of the Central Library." According to *Austin American-Statesman* reporter Wray Weddell in an article on August 15, 1951, "A request for a declaration of policy relating to use of the main City Library by Negroes was referred by the City Council Tuesday night to the City Library Commission, a citizens group."

In mid-September 1951, the City Library Commission recommended no change in the policy regarding use of the central library. The commission told Mayor Drake, "When a Negro borrower requests a book not available at the Carver Branch, the book is sent from the main library immediately." At a public meeting of the City Council, Kirk took strong exception to the commission's recommendations. Weddell wrote:

> In his argument Thursday, Kirk charged the library commission with recommending that "illegal administrative practices" be continued, and with admitting in its recommendations that the Negro library is not equal to the main facility. He said the commission's statement of equality "is entirely without foundation in fact." If they were equal it would not be necessary to send books from the main library to the Carver branch, he declared. He claimed that the commission recommended continuation of an illegal practice, by quoting what he said was a 1933 council amendment to an ordinance creating a library commission. The amendment, he said, provided that "nothing shall be done or practiced to limit the free use of the library or libraries by the public."
>
> [He] also quoted from what he said was a set of rules recommended by the library commission and adopted by the council in 1933. One of the rules, he said, "provided any resident or taxpayer of Austin shall be entitled to borrow books from the library by signing the proper application and agreement and receiving a borrower's card." The rule, Kirk declared, clearly indicates the council's intention that any citizen shall have free use of the library.[27]

Astor Kirk
(far right) with
future president
Lyndon B. Johnson
in the early 1960s
at a university
event. (The Dolph
Briscoe Center for
American History)

In reflecting some years later about enduring the process of integrating UT and challenging racialized city policy, Kirk came to the conclusion that his motivation was simply knowing "the fundamental truth that one cannot achieve and sustain wholeness of mind, body, and soul without forgiving those who inflict pain, cause misery, and sow seeds of discord, even when one is unable to forget what these others do." He was determined not to allow the Board of Regents and administrative officials of the university, the attorney general of Texas, and the print and broadcast media to control his story. "One of my basic objectives was to avoid giving them the tools with which to define me negatively. Most of the members of the faculty with whom I had relationships after I enrolled in the university in September 1950 were decent, honorable, ethical, and professional human beings. Because of the way I responded to those who had questioned me, they understood my motivation and end goal, and they treated me with respect, a respect I earned."

■ JOHN CHASE

In a sea of white faces, John Saunders Chase waited patiently amid the stares and glares of the swarm of humanity surrounding him. Cameras flashed as reporters hurled questions at him and jotted down his responses.

The road to the aforementioned moment began at an early age for John Chase. Although he knew what he wanted to do in life, he was, originally, at a loss to define it. "As a child, I loved to draw and to create things like buildings and airplanes," said Chase. "I knew what I loved to do but didn't really understand the concept of architecture until one day when I knocked on the front door of an architecture firm on West Street in Annapolis and told them I wanted to learn about what they did. Even though the members of the firm were white, they took me in and treated me like one of their own. They sat me at drafting tables and pulled out rolls of plans to show me. And, to this day, I am good friends with members of that firm."[28]

After high school, Chase followed in his sister's footsteps, enrolling at Hampton University in Virginia. "After graduating from Hampton I took a job in Philadelphia as a drafter. It was at that time that I began to realize just how few Black architects there were. Almost all of them were either in New York City or California." When Chase was offered a job in Austin with the Lott Lumber Company, he made his way to the trenches of the South in the spring of 1949. A welcome introduction to the world of architecture, the

Lott Company specialized in building houses and was owned by an African American family.[29]

Chase quickly realized that to pursue his passion and interests in architecture, he needed to advance his studies in the field. The best school for such a degree was the University of Texas at Austin, only a few miles from his home. While widely known for its academic reputation, it was equally known for its segregation. "But there wasn't any other college or university that you could go to in Austin that had architecture," Chase recalled, "so I decided to go and talk to the dean, Hugh McMath. I said 'Look, I'm from the East Coast, but I do understand the laws here, and they in essence say that you don't accept African Americans. I understand that, but I thought maybe it would be possible that I could somehow work a correspondence course.'" McMath responded with a conviction that foreshadowed major change on the horizon: "Are you familiar with the case that's in front of the Supreme Court as we speak?" McMath was speaking about *Sweatt v. Painter*. Chase had been made aware of the case and conflict months earlier, and while he too sought the opportunity to further his education, he conceded the role of pioneer to the more politically inclined. But with the encouragement of Dean McMath and with no agenda to politicize his pathway to higher education, Chase applied.[30]

John Chase registers for classes after standing in line among a crowd of students and journalists. (The Dolph Briscoe Center for American History)

A few weeks later Chase remembers the phone ringing off the hook at his house. The first call was from an Associated Press reporter. He said, "I guess you're aware of the situation at the Supreme Court, *Sweatt v. Painter*, and that you're now eligible for registration and admission to UT?" The reporter continued, "And I'm sure you're aware of the fact that the next chance to do that will be," and he named a date later in the summer session.[31] Chase recalls being emphatic in his response that he planned to be there on registration day. On June 7, 1950, Chase stood in line in Gregory Gym at UT Austin. Just two days earlier, the US Supreme Court had ruled in favor of desegregation in three separate civil rights cases. *McLaurin v. Oklahoma State* and *Henderson v. United States* focused on banning separate facilities at a university and prohibiting segregated seating arrangements on railroad cars, re-

spectively. The third case, *Sweatt v. Painter*, concerned equal education opportunities, specifically the right of Blacks to enroll in the School of Law at
the University of Texas. The court voted in favor of desegregation of graduate and professional schools, and the University of Texas at Austin became
the first major public university in the South to open its doors to Black graduate students.

Chase's enrollment at the university was in practice a political act, social
defiance, and a brave action, but in reality it merely reflected a man's thirst
for education and knowledge and professional aspiration. "I think I was just
too young to be afraid. I was concerned, but that's about all, I guess. But
we got tons of nasty letters. They were from various people around the state
and around the country who'd say, 'You should be ashamed of yourself, to
go somewhere that you're not wanted.' I didn't give a darn one way or another, but I did want some more ar-
chitecture. I really did." While aware
of them, Chase was not bothered by
his fellow students' opinions. Some
welcomed him, some ignored him,
and others admonished his presence.
And on that sweltering summer day
in June, he and Horace Lincoln
Heath became two of the first African Americans to enroll in graduate
studies at the University of Texas at
Austin.

Making it in the front door, however, did not promise a typical ma-
triculation into higher education or
the social experience often associated
with it. African Americans were not
allowed to live on campus; they were
not permitted to participate in college athletics and were restricted in
their socializing. The stadium was
segregated, as were the shops and res-

Chase sits in a
classroom on cam-
pus at UT Austin in
1950. (The Dolph
Briscoe Center for
American History)

taurants along Guadalupe Street. The Forty Acres in some ways functioned
like an incubator, massaging ideals of equality and change yet susceptible to
tainted perceptions of race, social capital, and fairness. In agreement with
the NAACP's assessment of racial attitudes in Texas, a student survey revealed that most white students were not offended by the presence of an African American student inside the classroom. And while Chase did not in-

tend to carry the banner for racial equality in enrolling at UT, he was keenly aware and conscious of his color and the impact his presence had on the campus and beyond. "Hampton was a predominantly Black institution, so I had never been in a classroom with white kids before," said Chase. "It was hard trying to focus on my studies as a graduate student while adjusting to an environment that was totally foreign to me."

"From the moment I set foot on the university campus, I was shadowed by federal marshals," said Chase. The completion of his degree was a transcendent moment for the institution and surely for those who might follow in his footsteps, but what often got lost in the narrative was the personal triumph it represented. "I waded through some waters up there that I had never been in before. I had no complaints other than the little sour things that every once in a while would pop up. In general, I think things went well. But Austin had a lot of problems," he said. Chase and his fellow Black pioneers on campus, such as Oscar L. Thompson, who entered UT in 1951 to achieve a master of science degree, received letters that read, "You are less than a dog to force your way into someplace that you're not wanted." Chase reflected, "You know stuff that people were not comfortable coming up to you and telling you face-to-face. They put it in a letter and sometimes signed it and sometimes not."[32]

Chase became the first African American to graduate from the university's School of Architecture, a journey he credits to a few caring professors. "I received a lot of hate mail using the 'N' word and a lot of passive-aggressive innuendos and undercuts, but I also received a lot of support from white friends and faculty who wanted to see me succeed." His triumph in the field of architecture was punctuated by the achievements taking place around campus by other Black scholars. Oscar L. Thompson in that same year is cited as being the first Black student to graduate from the university, after completing his thesis, "A Phenylthiocarbomide Taste Deficiency in a Negro." He would go on to become a staunch community leader and eventually served as a research assistant in the Human Genetics Foundation at the University of Texas at Austin, before he died of a heart attack in 1962.[33]

After receiving his master's degree in architecture, Chase was offered a position as an assistant professor at Texas Southern University (TSU) in Houston. He and his wife, Drucie, moved to Houston with great expectations of seeing his career as an architect blossom into a reality. Yet he faced continued discrimination in urban Houston. In interview after interview at architectural firms, Chase was denied employment. When he showed up to apply for a job, he was told there were no available openings. So Chase started his own business: "I thought to myself, if no one will hire you, you're going to take that state examination, pass it, and hire yourself," said Chase. "So that's

David Chapel
Missionary Baptist
Church, designed
by John Chase in
1950, is one of
Chases's many
iconic designs
in Austin, Texas.
(Texas Time Travel)

what I did. I hired myself." Having set a precedent for bypassing the social restrictions of his
time, in 1952 Chase passed the state examination and founded his own architectural firm.

Faced with inexperience and naïveté in
running a business, Chase drew on the education foundation he had developed at UT
and his daily cultural and racial interactions
in the surrounding college town. The subject of his master's thesis was "Progressive Architecture for Churches." "You see churches
were also still segregated. I realized that, if I
wanted business, I needed to approach the African American community. And the best way
to do that was to attend church. I figured I could learn how to build churches
with a little hard work and a lot of faith."[34] Chase managed to reinterpret
the effects of the oppressive Texas social conditions to inform a distinct business strategy and life model. Having helped open the door to the ivory tower
of the University of Texas for African Americans years earlier, he continued
his work, solidifying his legacy as a rule changer and social advocate, hiring
Black engineers, architects, and draftsmen in a field often unwelcoming to
their skill set, insight, and experience.

■ DORIS ASKEW-HICKS

The media in the 1940s carried many reports about the effort of Heman
Marion Sweatt to enter the law school at the University of Texas. In the
spring of 1947, Doris Alneitha Askew-Hicks was near the end of her junior
year in undergraduate school at Bishop College, an HBCU in Marshall,
Texas. Heman Sweatt had been invited to speak at his alma mater, nearby
Wiley College, about his effort to enter the UT Law School. Doris joined
about sixty other students from Bishop to hear him speak. "I admired him
for his effort, but I was sure that I would never attend a school where there
was that much opposition to my presence. My concern was, how could anyone learn in a hostile environment?"[35] A few years after that occasion at Wiley College, Sweatt was admitted to the law school. Doris, like many, admired and praised him from afar for his persistence, endurance, and bravery.

Two years after graduating from Bishop, Doris was employed as an elementary classroom teacher. She later made the decision to transition from
classroom teacher to school librarian. To aid her in that career choice, she

applied to Atlanta University School of Library Science in Atlanta, Georgia. "Most of the librarians I knew had graduated from the library school at Atlanta, and I was impressed by what they were doing in their profession and communities." Doris would spend only one summer there. While getting registered, she learned all the library school students from Texas were receiving out-of-state aid, which paid for all their expenses. "I was unaware of such a program, and it was too late to apply for aid that session, so I planned to begin immediately after the summer session to apply for the next summer session. I was truly looking forward to having the State of Texas pay for my education." Her application was denied, and she was informed that she would have to attend a library school in Texas before she would be eligible for out-of-state aid. That setback informed her decision to apply to the University of Texas. She was accepted. "I was fearful of the treatment I might receive at the university. I was somewhat motivated beyond my fear, when I discovered it would be much less costly to attend the University of Texas than to attend the Atlanta University School of Library Science."

Doris decided she would enroll only in the summer sessions so she could still work. It would not be financially feasible for her to take leave and be a full-time student. "I had to find housing outside the campus because the dormitories had not been opened to students of color." That created a transportation problem for Doris, so she had to arrange a carpool pickup every morning to get from the East Side to campus. "The first day at UT was overwhelming. There were long lines for registration. Everything big!" Doris's greatest surprise was the cost of registration. "I couldn't believe how little it cost." She would be paying less at UT than she would have if she had chosen to attend a smaller state-supported school designated for Black students. "I took the long walk and entered through one of those heavy double doors at the Tower. There were lots of people walking inside. I was looking for the elevator to go to the third floor where the library school was located and to meet with the director, when approached by a white man who introduced himself and offered to escort me to the elevator. He said, 'If I can assist you in any way, please don't hesitate to let me know.' I felt like he was sent by God to help me and end my fear and unease."

Later that same day, Doris met with the director of the library school. He greeted her with a smile and a handshake and offered her a chair. After a few general remarks he asked, "Why did you choose this school?" Doris replied that she wanted a degree in library science from an accredited school. "How long do you think it will take?" he followed up. "I have no time line. I will be attending summers only," she replied. He smiled and gave her an overview of the program and the demands. He then offered some advice about how to pace herself and survive the rigorous program. She soon met all of her teachers and a few other Black students, some of whom had entered the library school earlier. "I ended that day feeling more comfortable with my decision to come to UT."

The library school was almost self-contained, so the first two summer sessions, Doris rarely had to go elsewhere on the campus for resources. The only contact she had with other students from other schools was in the Commons, where she took at least one meal every day. "I can remember hearing the 'N' word once. It was in the Commons where someone was talking about an incident that had happened elsewhere. I remember not being surprised but uncomfortable at the ease in which the word was thrown away." Beyond that incident and other exposures to ignorant rhetoric, Doris got along just fine with the other white students in her program. And if they were not friendly, they just simply ignored her. Some of her most uncomfortable moments involved the brutally hot library. "The atmosphere was very conducive for studying except for the lack of air conditioning. The fans helped, but they were circulating hot air." Other than the climate conditions, Doris not only academically thrived but took on roles among her peers that demonstrated in some ways progress and potential for true integration. "The library school had an organization for students, I don't recall the name, but I do remember that we would gather around food to get to know our professors and fellow students and paid a small amount for dues. I was elected the treasurer. I was excited that I was trusted by my peers to oversee the money. It may seem small, but it meant something." Doris completed her degree by attending consecutive summer sessions. The summer also played host to the annual Texas State Library Association meetings. The school always had a banquet at the annual meetings, which she attended. When she arrived at a meeting one summer, the young woman checking her in stated her concern that she was at the wrong building. Doris stood there perplexed by her assessment until some of her white schoolmates saw her and greeted her with a hug. "The woman just stood there in awe. Every time I looked at her she was staring at me."

Despite Doris's overwhelmingly positive experience at UT, instances like this provided stark doses of reality of what her presence meant to the cultural, social, and political landscape of UT. She and her Black peers would instigate institutional change, but that change would be subject to individual resistance.

The summer session offered all the required courses that were offered during the regular sessions, but there was less time to do them. For Doris that meant she had little time for extracurricular activities. "Some students said that I worked too hard, but I worked hard because that was what was required of me in order to meet the grade standards. I was surrounded by students, mostly white, who came from greater and richer educational opportunities." In Doris's estimation her white peers were better prepared than she was.

She said, "I look back at my time at the university fondly. I feel it gave me the best opportunity to prepare for a rewarding career as a school librarian. According to the high evaluations I received throughout my career, the school did an excellent job preparing me for all the positions I held."

Doris largely credited her time at UT for the recognition and experiences she attained throughout her career. In 1959, she received a master of library science (MLS) degree and had a long career in New York, after she and her husband were both recruited to work in Rochester. A principal of a blue-ribbon high school requested Doris be placed in his school; she was eventually promoted to director of the Department of Learning Resources. She remained in that position for eight years, during which time she was appointed by the president of the university and commissioner of education for the State of New York to serve a three-year term on a new state advisory council. "I retired in 1981 at age fifty-five feeling that I had an enjoyable and successful career because I had been prepared at GSLIS [Graduate School of Library and Information Sciences] to meet the challenges and contribute to the profession and make a valuable difference in the lives of young people. I remain amazed at the opportunities that I had and the successes I experienced." She added, "I'm not sure I would have been that prepared had I attended any other school."

Doris was never able to confirm that she was the first Black student in the UT GSLIS program, although she remembers being the only one at the time. "I have been told there is no proof from the registration office at the University of Texas because they do not keep a record of graduates by race; however, I was told by the director of the School of Library and Information Science, Dr. Robert Raymond Douglas; my adviser, Dr. Esther Stallmann; and my teachers that I was the first African American to graduate from GSLIS." UT's first would help transform the lives of school children across the country.

CHAPTER TWO

Negotiating a Space for Blackness on Campus and Beyond

SITUATED IN THE HEART OF the capital city of Texas, by the 1950s UT had proven itself to be one of the state's premier public institutions of education. Such a status demanded strong leadership, conservative infrastructure, and unprecedented actions to attract students, funds, and support from around the state. UT's campus is barely more than a mile north of the State Capitol building, but spatially oriented in such a way that it often seemed like a self-contained community, especially in the 1950s when the campus was not as sprawling as it is today. "The Drag," Guadalupe Street, which runs alongside the university from Nineteenth to Twenty-Sixth Streets (now Martin Luther King Jr. Boulevard and Dean Keeton Street, respectively), provided the approximately eighteen thousand students with their own shopping and eating areas. The students were predominantly white, middle class, and participants in a social life that revolved around football games in the fall, Barton Springs in the spring, and proms, beauty contests, and sorority and fraternity events throughout the school year. They were comfortable in their roles as students and in their potential future as leading citizens (or the wives of leading citizens) in the state of Texas. Such privileged idealism was evident inside the Forty Acres and unchallenged in the Austin community.

East Avenue (now Interstate Highway 35) was the city's dividing line. Once you crossed it, there stood another Austin, a different social existence, a predominantly Black and Latino community created a few decades earlier, as the result of the city-mandated migration known as the City Plan of 1928. The plan forced Blacks to move to the eastern part of town if they wanted access to city services—including utilities and education. Segregation permeated Austin's social, political, and educational infrastructures. Although UT Austin students were recognized as being somewhat liberal and "largely sympathetic to Black civil rights, they were only vaguely familiar with issues," according to historian Michael Gillette.[1] Civil rights activist Astor Kirk, a faculty member at Huston-Tillotson College who had applied to UT Austin to attend graduate school and was denied admission prior to the decision

A Black student holds a sign that reads, "Is Austin Progressive?" The poster was presumably part of a student protest about the treatment and social integration of Black students at UT Austin. (Texas Student Publications Collection)

in *Sweatt v. Painter*, was asked during a 1984 interview if Blacks were treated better in Austin than elsewhere in Texas. He replied, "Basically yes in the sense that the white intelligentsia here . . . were more open than what I found in Houston and Dallas and to some extent San Antonio." But he added, "They did recognize what the system was, and they probably did not have the courage to behave in ways that were consistent with their own beliefs."[2]

Thus, Austin's Black residents attended their own schools on the city's East Side, which included L. C. Anderson High School and Kealing Junior High, as well as several elementary schools and the private historically Black college, Huston-Tillotson College (now Huston-Tillotson University), an HBCU established by the Lutheran Church. Black residents could ride buses to the western side of town, primarily to work as domestics in the homes of white people, but were guided by the unwritten laws that mandated they sit in the back of the bus, not use the dressing rooms at the stores where they purchased clothing, or be served at the restaurants or coffee shops they passed along the way. Such social practices were exacerbated by limited access to the city's primary institution of higher education. This social conduct would also become the norm and expectation of those few Black students who found themselves enrolled at UT. The campus would become a microcosmic representation of the city and country's racialization of space and place.

In 1956, when the first Black undergraduates were admitted to UT, the Board of Regents could legally argue that the university was integrated, but the legality of desegregation only enforced certain policies and supported particular spaces and practices. While Black students were permitted to attend classes at UT, they faced inequality as part of their lived experience outside the classroom. Under the headline, "One Big 'Cannot'—A Negro Student's Life," an article published in the *Daily Texan* in 1960, pointed out that Black students "couldn't take part in campus drama productions, intercollegiate sports, or enter some Drag establishments. . . . They had to use segregated bathrooms in Memorial Stadium. . . . They couldn't join Interfraternity or Panhellenic Council."[3]

As some students noted, UT was desegregated but certainly not integrated. Black students were far from achieving the social normalcy of collegiate life or taking part in the cultural landscape of Austin. It was clear to many students of color that opportunities for social engagement, cultural affirmation, and collegiate entertainment would not be created or nurtured by the university. Such support would have to be cultivated by students and the help of the Black Austin community, mostly concentrated on the East Side. Although students were angry and resentful that they were not afforded the same experience as their white counterparts, they were committed to developing important and influential cultural institutions that ultimately became mechanisms for individual and collective preservation.

For many Black students, the conversation started with housing accommodations. Black students were not permitted to live on campus, further isolating them from campus life and limiting opportunities for social inclusion. The push for housing for Black students had become a major concern of both the UT stu-

A young Black woman in the early 1960s holds a sign in protest. (Texas Student Publications Collection)

A Black student walks the streets of Austin during a protest. (Texas Student Publications Collection)

dents and the administration. While UT had opened up avenues for Black students to earn a degree from the university, ongoing bias, social concerns, and political pressures all but removed Black presence on campus. However, housing was not the only concern. The full quality of life for Black students on the Forty Acres was called into question. Black students were demanding not just equal housing options but a full college experience. To ensure that they would both survive the UT experience and have the potential to thrive, the UT administration had to consider offering more than a classroom education. UT would have to provide access to all the amenities to which white students were entitled on campus and on the Drag. Black students would eventually demand the opportunity to attend the movie theaters, get a cup of coffee or a meal in the cafés and restaurants, have their hair cut in the barbershops, and purchase school supplies and clothing from the campus Co-op. In other words, they wanted to be able to participate in all the commercial and social activities that were considered an integral part of campus life.

■ INTEGRATING THE DRAG

Students and others who favored desegregation started their protests by picketing the restaurants on the Drag and the lunch counters on Congress Avenue in downtown Austin.[4] Although Black students could eat at university cafeterias and one privately owned restaurant, the UT venues were closed on the weekends, leaving those students no place to get a meal in the campus area. To confront this problem, in the early 1960s students from UT and Huston-Tillotson took part in sit-ins at lunch counters downtown. They were peaceful; when Blacks were asked to leave, they got up and left, but as soon as they did, others took their places. In an exhibit of photos from the diner era, the Austin History Center noted, "Sit-ins effectively brought attention to the injustices of segregation and helped turn the tide of public opinion during the Civil Rights movement."[5]

Black and white students gather at a restaurant on the Drag to protest for the right for all residents and students to eat at the establishment. (Texas Student Publications Collection)

The Tally Ho Restaurant located on the Drag posts a sign on the front door that reads, "We reserve the right to refuse service to anyone." These signs were often posted on establishments on the Drag and throughout Austin to discourage and intimidate students and residents of color. (Texas Student Publications Collection)

The first restaurant on the Drag to integrate was the Night Hawk, a popular hamburger place owned by Harry Akin. Akin, who later became a mayor of Austin, set the tone for other diners and restaurants in the city. In 1963, he was one of one hundred restaurant representatives from Southern states who attended a conference in Washington, D.C., hosted by Attorney General Robert Kennedy. As Akin reported, "Kennedy urged us to do whatever we could in our respective communities as quickly as possible toward integrating our restaurants on a voluntary basis in the interest of avoiding dangerous racial situations in this country."[6]

The following month, Akin brought together representatives of eighteen Austin restaurants and hotels to sign a resolution in which they agreed to desegregate their food establishments immediately. He believed that collective action among a coalition of restaurant owners would prove to be more effective.[7] In the beginning, many restaurants in the city said they would close their doors if sit-ins were started.[8]

Next, students redirected their efforts to integrating theaters on the Drag. While this was an attempt to address entertainment amenities for Black students, it also had academic imperatives for some. Many students recounted that faculty members occasionally assigned their students to view movies related to their course work. Chandler Davidson, now a professor emeritus at Rice University, was influential in leading the fight to integrate theaters on the Drag by organizing demonstrations in front of the Varsity and Texas theaters. Beginning in January 1962, with the support of white students as well as some faculty and friends, they held stand-ins at the theaters. Within a month, some five hundred students and others had joined in. For nearly a year, hundreds of students participated in the protests. Some of the students also played antisegregation games. For example, two or three Blacks would dress as students from Saudi Arabia and in that way were permitted entry to theaters with no questions asked.[9] Another ploy was for whites to approach the theater box office and ask if the theater sold tickets to all Americans. When the answer was yes, they would bring forth a Black student to buy a ticket. When that student was refused, the group would leave and another group would take its place.[10] First, Blacks were admitted to the balconies, which were designated for "colored only." Finally, in 1961, Blacks were admitted to the two theaters, with the proviso that everyone who purchased tickets must show student identification. At that same time, the downtown theaters remained closed to Blacks.[11] In addition, 260 faculty members showed their

White and Black students protest continued discriminatory policies at the theater on the drag. (Texas Student Publications Collection)

UT students protest on the Drag, a street that runs parallel to the university campus and was known for its local restaurants, theater, and clothing stores, most of which were open only to white patrons. (Texas Student Publications Collection)

support by signing a four-column ad in the *Austin American-Statesman* endorsing theater integration.[12]

■ FORMING BLACK GREEK LIFE

Banned from joining athletic teams and university clubs and forbidden from entering the theaters and restaurants along the Drag, the earliest of Black undergraduates at the University of Texas at Austin had few social outlets. But determined to make a life at the university, UT's first Black students got to work forming their own social clubs, and within a year, the underpinnings of intercollegiate Greek fraternities and sororities were in place.

It was 1956, and first-year student Mamie Hans Ewing (then Mamie Hans) remembers meeting with a group of professional women at the Eliza Dee Hall, located on the campus of Samuel Huston College (now Huston-Tillotson University)—the only dormitory available to UT's Black female students at the time. The women, who were a mix of physicians, professionals, and college professors, shared one thing—they were all members of Alpha Kappa Alpha (AKA) Sorority, Inc., and members of the Beta Psi Omega Austin graduate chapter. "They asked us if we had anyone in our family who belonged to any sororities," Hans Ewing said. "At that time in the 1950s most of us did not, so they started to talk to us about starting a chapter of AKA at the University of Texas." Soon thereafter the women launched an interest group called "The Vine Club."[13]

Similarly, on the other side of I-35, a group of African American males launched their own social club formed by Alpha Phi Alpha brothers who had transferred into the university from other HBCUs. Like AKA, they launched a social club, Alpha Upsilon Tau (AUT or Alpha at UT), becoming the first to formally do so in the fall of 1957.

One of the club's founding members was Walter C. Jones, who had previously studied at the Tuskegee Institute but transferred to UT to obtain an accredited architecture degree. "I had become an Alpha at Tuskegee, and I came to UT and met other Alphas, and we realized we had that common relationship," Jones said. "And so we decided to start working on the charter. At that point the university was pretty much segregated. You couldn't play football; there were no African Americans playing any sports when we first came. Same goes for going to the movies. The only thing that was acceptable for us at that point was the church."[14]

Jones and his peers, known as the "Chapter Organizers," authored a letter to Alpha Phi Alpha, and on April 24, 1958, they were granted recognition as a chapter. In partnership with the Austin Alpha Phi Alpha graduate chap-

Above, members of the UT chapters of Omega Psi Phi fraternity and, below, Alpha Phi Alpha fraternity in the late 1960s. (The Dolph Briscoe Center for American History, Almetris Mama Duren Private Collection)

ter, Gamma Eta Lambda, as well as with assistance from the Delta chapter of Huston-Tillotson, the Chapter Organizers filled their first pledge class. Still under its probationary period, these initial pledges entered into what was known as the Sphinx Club (the sphinx is the fraternity's symbol). On December 12, 1958, the first line of Epsilon Iota, composed of twelve men, "crossed the burning sands" and were initiated into the fraternity. On March 5, 1960, the fraternity received its official charter and was formally installed as the Epsilon Iota chapter of Alpha Phi Alpha Incorporated.

Although Alpha Phi Alpha is recognized as the first Greek organization to start the charter process at UT Austin, it was not the first to actually obtain a charter. The Delta Xi chapter of Alpha Kappa Alpha holds that honor, having incorporated its charter line of fifteen members at high noon on May 16, 1959, in the Queen Ann Room in the Texas Union.

"Oh, we took particular pride in being first, as did the soros of Beta Psi Omega [the AKA Austin chapter founded in 1938]," Hans Ewing said. "These [Beta Psi Omega soros] were accomplished women who had primarily been initiated on historically black college campuses. They took immense pride in AKA being first—it was more pride in being first than being in the sorority." In addition to local members, Hans Ewing said that Regional Directors Eugene Long and Besselle Atwell as well as members from the national AKA office were on hand for their initiation.[15]

Beyond social aspects, the early African American Greek organizations also served as support systems. Looking back, first-line Alpha brother Emanuel McKinney said some of his fondest memories are of the relationship he and his brothers shared during the fraternity's infancy. "It was pretty obvious that the environment at the university was really not great, undesirable so to speak," McKinney said. "Just to be able to assist in making college life as enjoyable as it could be under the discriminatory environment [where] we found ourselves, that was part of the purpose we served in addition to the bond of being fraternity brothers."[16]

Likewise, Hans Ewing said AKA provided her a similar sense of family and togetherness. "In the 1950s at the University of Texas, where we were ignored and looked upon without any favor, it was very nice to have a group of women to be our support system," she said. "It was comforting to have

Members of the UT chapter of AKA in the late 1970s. (The Dolph Briscoe Center for American History, Almetris Mama Duren Private Collection)

a group of people you had something in common with." The AKAs also bonded through community service, much of which took place at a local nursing home as well as the Wesley United Methodist and St. James Episcopal Churches in East Austin.[17]

Hans Ewing, who would later become the graduate adviser of the UT Austin AKAs, also holds the Beta Psi Omega soros in particular regard for

Members of the Alpha fraternity and the Delta sorority laugh at a gathering in the early 1970s. (The Dolph Briscoe Center for American History, Almetris Mama Duren Private Collection)

The Delta Sigma Theta chapter formed on March 26, 1960, and continues to have an active presence on campus and in the Austin community.

what they went through to see that the UT Austin chapter was formed. "These women who came on campus to try to get this done couldn't even drink out of the water fountains and walked into a very segregated environment," she said. "However, these Alpha Kappa Alpha women persisted."[18]

McKinney and his other Alpha brothers are proud of all they were able to accomplish, being associated with the beginning of something that lasts, as he put it. "It gives you a sense of pride and accomplishment and joy that in some small way you have contributed to something that is still going on and helping to make this, even if just in some small way, a better society."[19]

■ CONNECTING TO THE EAST SIDE

Students were not just relegated to the racialized policies of UT or those businesses in proximity to the school. There were other social and cultural institutions throughout the city that prohibited Black presence. Churches, too, were segregated.

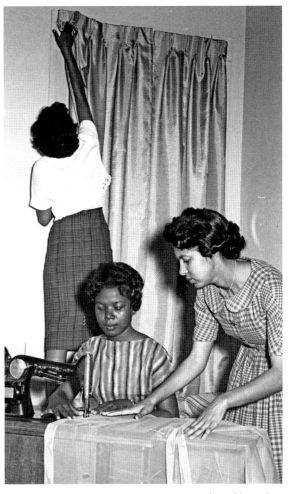

Students like Walta Marie Smith (right) who lived in Whitis Co-op furnished and decorated their rooms, often with donations from East Austin residents and churches. (The Dolph Briscoe Center for American History, Almetris Mama Duren Private Collection)

The first to end that practice in the campus area was Dr. Blake Smith, pastor of the University Baptist Church. According to a longtime church member, Smith announced that his church would be integrated. This split the membership right down the middle. At the next deacons' meeting, the vote was six in favor of integration and six opposed, necessitating a vote by the chair. The chair, an elderly gentleman, prefaced his vote with this explanation: "I don't like niggers. I don't want a nigger sitting by me in church. But I don't think it's what I want but what God wants. I vote to integrate and to keep Blake Smith."[20]

Under Smith's guidance, the church first admitted Blacks to worship in the late 1940s and shortly thereafter admitted them as members. Those who could not tolerate the idea of Black members left the church. However, Dr. Smith and others in the church continued their policy, leading to the ouster of the church from the Austin Baptist Association (ABA). In time,

In Austin, the strategy to isolate minorities came in the form of the Koch and Fowler City Plan, which in 1928 proposed the creation of a "Negro District," making it the only part of the city where African Americans could access schools and other public services. Architects Koch and Fowler also proposed that the district have the city's weakest zoning restrictions, allowing the development of "a number of slightly objectionable industrial uses"— essentially, any use that was not specifically outlawed. (Koch and Fowler City Plan, 1928; Tretter, *Austin Restricted*)

however, the ABA reinstated the church.[21] In 1958, Bishop John E. Hines of the Episcopal Diocese of Texas called for racial integration and equality in local churches as well as in Episcopal schools and camps.[22] In 1963, the Austin Council of Churches adopted a resolution "commending generally the progress of integration in the city in recent weeks." They called on the churches "to take a bold forthright stand" on integration in the city's churches.[23]

Throughout the 1950s and 1960s, the city was setting up organizations to aid in desegregation of its facilities. One was the Austin Equal Citizenship Corporation, a nonprofit group set up "to promote and encourage, by all lawful means, appreciation of and respect for" all racial, ethnic, and nationality groups living in Austin. Another was the Human Opportunities Corporation, an agency of the Community Action Program. From 1954 to 1970, "it brought together for the first time representatives of Austin's three major ethnic groups to plan and administer various community action programs funded by the Johnson administration's War on Poverty."[24] In addition to churches, other City of Austin amenities were being opened to Blacks. Most notable among them were Barton Springs, the city's famous natural springs pool; the public libraries; and the municipal golf course. Minutes of the Austin Equal Citizenship Corporation of February 8, 1967, revealed that three banks employed Negroes or Latin Americans as clerks and that two hospitals, Brackenridge and Holy Cross, had totally integrated staffs.

However, it seems many in Austin were oblivious to the effects of segregation. As a student in the 1950s pointed out, "For most whites at the time, the injustice was not apparent. For most it was not a matter of bigotry or hatred; they were decent, good people. It was just the way things were."[25] Chandler Davidson, who organized Students for Direct Action, noted that "most of the students are not even aware of the segregation tactics employed by the University and by business firms in the campus area." He considered integration "practically at a standstill in the University area."[26]

After the initial integration of UT by a handful of pioneers like John Chase and Heman Sweatt, admitted African American graduate students looked to external resources to help navigate the choppy waters of academic and social life around campus. Despite the pervasiveness of institutionalized racism throughout the state, Blacks in Austin established a vibrant, thriving community in the eastern part of the city. A number of independent, Black-owned businesses were established there. In East Austin lay a close-knit Black community, including the only higher education resource available to students of color, Huston-Tillotson. In a twist of irony, the school's roots run deeper than those of the University of Texas. Opening its doors in 1877 as Tillotson Collegiate and Normal Institute, the school began classes on January 17, 1881. The University of Texas did not formally open until 1883. It was necessary to create an all-Black institution because the Texas Constitution of 1876 required segregated schools. The historically Black institution in East Austin became Huston-Tillotson after the 1952 merger of two colleges birthed out of the American Missionary Society of Congregational Churches. The small campus would become a shelter and a haven for Black students at UT, serving to supplement the lack of support and understanding of UT faculty and administration alike during the first few decades of UT's integration era.

Women standing outside the Austin Equal Citizenship Corporation in the late 1950s. (Travis County Negro Extension Program, May 24, 1960, at Austin History Center, courtesy of *Austin American-Statesman*)

This aerial photo of East Avenue in the 1950s shows the divide between East Austin and West Austin, which ultimately separated Black students from a social life on campus. (Texas Department of Transportation)

CHAPTER THREE

Overcoming the Odds

ALTHOUGH UT HAD OPENED its doors to black students, it was made clear that the extent of Black student life would be restricted to the classroom. Many of the regents and members of the UT community believed that an education in its purest form was the only obligatory service UT owed any of the Black students. Personal development, social integration, or campus involvement was not promised or provided.

During a 2010 convening of the Precursors, many of the first generation of African American students shared memories of their social experience in the early years. Many agreed that their first year or two on campus was merely an attempt to survive. With the opportunity to attend UT came a sense of responsibility. While it was a personal journey, many of the students understood that their experience was a wider reflection of the African American narrative in Texas and Southern education practices. Heman Sweatt once wrote in an article for the *Texas Ranger* in support of his lawsuit against Texas: "It cannot be denied that the implications of this matter are destined to affect the lives of many other Negroes. But I am responsible only to the extent of my application."[1] The consequences of their success or failure had an immense ripple effect that was surely understood by students and the community. Thus, regardless of circumstance, the struggle to survive the Forty Acres became a community effort driven by determined students and reinforced by community investment in what was possible moving forward.

■ DOROTHY CATO

In May 1965, Dorothy Cato (formerly Dorothy Green) was named valedictorian of her graduating class at Edwards High, an all-Black, segregated school in Gonzales, Texas. The distinction of being valedictorian, alongside a scholarship from the Gonzales Music Study Club, afforded her the opportunity to receive a scholarship for tuition and fees from a state college or university.

Dorothy came from a long line of farmers and sharecroppers, and the importance of hard work was instilled in her from an early age. She would often work with her father on the land in rural Elm Slough, experiencing firsthand the labor that it required. The land in Elm Slough, known as a Freedom Colony, was purchased by her mother's grandfather. "Later, we moved away from the farm, after my parents secured jobs in the nearby town of Gonzales, Texas. My father continued to farm the land part time. My mother secured a teaching job at Riverside Elementary School and taught in various schools for forty-six years. My parents, Warren and Mary Green, were my greatest role models."[2]

It was this example set by her parents that made the pursuit of college both an obligation and a luxury. All of her siblings graduated from college, three of them from Prairie View College (now University), and became teachers. The other three graduated and worked in the medical field. The bar had been set, and Dorothy would not only meet the expectations and standards of her family but set a precedent for her entire community. Although small, Gonzales was still majority white and suffered the same racial segregation and inequality of most Texas and Southern cities. But at the age of seventeen, Dorothy would commit to attending the University of Texas at Austin, becoming the first African American from the small town of Gonzales to be admitted to UT.

Dorothy arrived at UT, honored by the opportunity to represent her family and town and hopeful she would manage to balance expectations in the classroom and the overwhelming shift to life on campus. Unfortunately, the state scholarship she earned did not include housing at UT. "Living off campus was really the only option I had. An apartment or co-op was what was left for those of us non-oil-money kids," she said.

Dorothy came to Austin the summer before classes started with her parents to find a place for her to live. They ultimately ended up at Huston-Tillotson College (HT). Met with support and direction at HT, the family was referred to a large, white house at 1209 East Twelfth Street, which was home to female students from both HT and UT. Fortunately, there was still a room available. As classes began at UT for the fall semester, Dorothy found herself packing a lunch and making sure she was at the bus stop promptly by 6:00 a.m. to make her 8:00 a.m. class. This is what was required of her and many other Black students: long, early-morning and late-night bus expeditions to claim an education at UT. The bus first traveled downtown to Twelfth Street and Congress. From there, Dorothy transferred to a bus traveling north to Guadalupe, or the "Drag." The pressure to arrive at the bus stop on time in the morning and make sure she left campus at a safe hour after an evening of studying caused stress. However difficult the circumstances

WOMEN'S
CO-OPERATIVES

winning the Texas Union Carving Contest with the happiest
pumpkin. Large Thanksgiving and Christmas dinners were
held for many college men. Fire drills, in addition to regularly scheduled house meetings, were conducted throughout
the year.

Dr. Dorothy Cato (seated on 2nd row, 4th from the left) in 1964 with the women of the
Whitis Co-op, later affectionately referred to as the Almetris Co-op. The co-op served as
some Black women's only housing option before dormitories on campus were integrated
in 1965 and as a vital support system for many Black students. (*Cactus* Yearbook, the
University of Texas at Austin)

proved to be, Dorothy was prepared and persistent. She had been dutifully
taught by her parents to lean on her faith in God and the support system of
community.

Although she was managing the less-than-ideal situation, about halfway
into the fall semester, she began to ask other Black students about their housing arrangements. She eventually learned about the Almetris Co-op. Encouraged by the proximity of the co-op to the UT campus and by the reputation
of the housemother, Almetris Duren, Dorothy's parents came to Austin to
make a formal introduction and tour the co-op. "I remember Ms. Duren as
a warm, slender woman with a welcoming smile and graying hair. By far, the
most heartfelt person you could meet," Dorothy said. She recalls the day she
met with Duren and requested room and board at the co-op. Duren initially
said there were no rooms available, as it was the middle of the fall semester,
but true to her reputation she made it work. "Ms. Duren asked us to wait for
a moment as she went upstairs. After a few moments, she returned and invited my parents and myself upstairs to a screened-in porch. As we walked
upstairs, Ms. Duren mentioned that if the student living on the porch, Margaret "Peaches" Ellis, did not mind sharing, she could offer me a place to
stay." As it turned out, Dorothy knew the student in question; they had become acquainted in high school as part of an honors organization called the
New Homemakers of America. A bed, bedding, and other essentials were located, and the screened-in porch became not only Dorothy's bedroom but a
symbol of the community she would have around her for the next four years.

After moving into the co-op, Dorothy no longer had to take the bus at

Dorothy Cato (top row, 5th from left) listed as a member of the Delta Sigma Theta, during the sorority's first few years as an official chapter on campus. (*Cactus* Yearbook, the University of Texas at Austin)

6:00 a.m.; she could literally walk to classes and the library as well as have a more active campus life. "I joined several service organizations and a sorority, Delta Sigma Theta, Inc. Looking back on it, I really enjoyed campus life. Although UT didn't offer us everything, we made our own spaces for social enrichment; we made a life for Black students on campus."

There were approximately eighteen to twenty girls living in the co-op. It was both cost-effective and what Dorothy described as "an oasis in a sea of white." It comprehensively met the needs of the young women, providing shelter, structure, and a social outlet. Girls were assigned duty areas, either cooking or cleaning, which reduced the cost of living for everyone. The women in the co-op were expected to contribute and help cultivate an ethos of family and community. But the Almetris Co-op was not just a place of enrichment for Black women; Mama Duren became a mother to Black men as well. "The guys were welcome most nights of the week to join us for dinner. She'd divvy up the tasks; someone made the vegetables, the meat, the bread, and others set the table. The guys would trek from the Alpha house or the men's barracks to our house and yell 'man on the hall' when they entered." Dinner was often followed by a game of cards or an impromptu therapy session with Mama Duren discussing the happenings of the day or the latest news. Mama Duren made it her business to know everybody's business, tracking not only the academic progress of each of her girls but their relationship status as well. "She was the mama that looked out [for us]. The guys felt just as indebted to Mama Duren as we did. . . . She had a way of making us feel special, protected, and like family," Dorothy recalled.

And as family is, Mama Duren as matriarch was very protective of the girls. This meant setting curfew for all co-op members and serving as liaison between Black students and the UT administration. "She'd earned UT's trust, and she was our biggest advocate." In 1966, after years of criticism and months of protest, the dormitories were opened to Black students. Despite the option to assimilate into white life on campus, Dorothy chose to stay at Almetris Co-op all four years of her undergraduate studies. Life at the Almetris Co-op was a balance of family, community, and real life. "It was a safety net, one I hung closely to. We had regularly scheduled house meetings to address any concerns both within the co-op and in the world. You can imagine that in the early 1960s there was plenty to talk about politically and socially," Dorothy said. Duren created a space that was not only a safe haven from the stresses of the classroom but a forum for working through the often intense discourse concerning race and place on campus and in the United States. "Living at Almetris Co-op with Ms. Duren and the other girls felt like family."

In 1969, Dorothy was awarded a bachelor of music education degree and began a career in teaching. Twenty years later she returned to the Forty Acres to pursue her master's in education and later earn her PhD. Dorothy's contribution to the UT story was recognized in 2014 by the Texas Exes Black Alumni Network with the Unsung Service Award. When discussing the award and her time at UT, Dorothy reflects: "I am forever indebted to Ms. Duren for making room for me. Her legacy lives on through the students' lives and their families. She touched many souls through the years. I believe Ms. Duren was the guardian angel for African American students at UT. I believed she was my angel, and her presence truly and greatly contributed to my success."

■ RODNEY GRIFFIN

When Rodney Griffin came to the University of Texas at Austin in 1965, African Americans were allowed to live on campus, eat in the cafeteria, join a student organization—even participate in college sports. On paper, the university leveled the field for all students. Yet for Griffin and his few classmates of color, segregation was alive and well on campus.

During the height of the Black Power movement, Griffin navigated the turbulent waters of social and political change on the Forty Acres and in the community. His standout college memories involve marches and picketing demonstrations—even jail time for civil disobedience. "It was a transformative era," says Griffin, who earned his bachelor's degree in math in 1970.[3] "Malcolm X was coming onto the scene, the cultural nationalist movement was on the rise, and we were asking, 'Who are we? Is this a change we want? Do we want to be carbon copies of white folks and the values they represent? What does it mean to be Black?'"

Plagued by these questions, Griffin wanted to know how other African American Longhorns were feeling at a university where they represented just 1 percent of the student population. As luck would have it, a friend referred him to a psychology professor who was in need of a research assistant with great people skills who could interview seventy Black students about their experiences on campus. He got the job and successfully completed his field-work. The findings, featured in a 1969 *Daily Texan* story, were quite telling but not surprising, Griffin says.

"The study gave a good panoramic view of what was felt from a Black per-spective," says Griffin. "The bottom line: Black students didn't feel at home or comfortable. It was apparent that if the university didn't take action to make life better for Black students, it could be facing another Cornell."

UT students protest the social climate for students of color on the UT campus in 1968. (Texas Student Publications Collection)

By "another Cornell" he is referencing a watershed day in US higher education when a large group of gun-toting mem-bers of the Afro-American Society occu-pied Willard Straight Hall to protest Cor-nell University's discriminatory policies and its slow progress toward establishing a Black studies program. Given the state of social and political unrest, Griffin's survey results came at an opportune time. The university's Ethnic Minority Affairs Com-mittee provided UT Austin president Nor-man Hackerman with eleven demands for correcting the university's racial inequali-ties. Informed by the survey, the president put a plan in motion to improve campus life for students of color.

Griffin says the aftermath of the survey was a pivotal point in UT Austin history, but not a watershed moment. He gives that honor to his older sister, Sherryl Grif-fin Bozeman, who—along with fellow stu-dents Maudie Ates and Leroy Sanders and the girls' fathers, Monroe Ates and Wil-liam Griffin—filed a lawsuit against UT in 1961 that led to the integration of its res-idence halls. It was a historic triumph that directly impacted the lives of Af-rican American students, Griffin says.

Yet not all victories resulted in immediate action. The eleven demands that stemmed from his study took years—decades even—to see light of day. "The irony of those eleven demands is that none were ever met immediately," Grif-fin notes. "However, they were the antecedents of what you now see at UT, such as the John L. Warfield Center for African and American Studies or the

Department of African and African Diaspora Studies." With the creation of several multicultural centers and departments, the university has seen a great deal of progress over the years, Griffin says, but notes the journey to equality is not over yet. "The racial issue has not been fixed yet," Griffin says. "Equity has not been achieved, but I believe we're on the right path. University leaders need to speed it up, drop the word 'incremental' from their vocabulary, and listen to folks in the community who have resolutions to these issues and get it done."

Long before UT Austin's Division of Diversity and Community Engagement was created, Griffin was carrying out its vision to extend the university's intellectual resources to the Austin community and empower underserved residents to take on leadership positions at the local and national levels. During his career as a curriculum writer at Southwest Educational Development Laboratory in Austin, Griffin met John L. Warfield, an esteemed professor of educational psychology and director of the Center for African and African American Studies in the College of Liberal Arts. Together they worked on a number of projects to benefit the community. "We met and started working on this whole notion of community engagement—bringing UT into dispossessed communities," Griffin adds. "John, whom we liked to call 'Brother John,' had strong leadership skills—the kind of skills the East Austin community needed. He could channel anger into constructive energy for community building."

Inspired by Warfield's leadership, Griffin dedicates his career to social change. He is a member of the Precursors, Inc., a group of alumni who are among the first Black students to attend and integrate UT Austin more than forty years ago. As a member of this group, he works to ensure that future generations of Black students are supported at the university. He is also an executive member of the state Democratic Party.

The proudest accomplishment in life, he says, is the one that has not come yet. "My proudest moment will be when Black students at UT are represented at the same percentage as they are in Texas high schools," he says. "It hasn't come yet, but I will continue to be working and watching until it happens."

■ **FRED ALEXANDER**

Fred Alexander knew early on in his life that he wanted to explore design and the development of buildings. As a teenager he sketched automobiles as a hobby and was drawn to the study of their aesthetic and functionality. Before graduating from high school in 1960, he made a decision to stay in Texas, which in his estimation meant he would have to forgo any plans to pursue automobile or industrial design because that would inevitably require studying and working out of state. To his knowledge there were not many programs in that field accessible to African Americans. UT was one of the few schools in the state that offered a design-related major and was open to Black enrollment. "Even though segregation was still a fact of life in Texas and to a great extent at UT, I knew that changes were coming and that as a young Black Texan, I should take advantage of the opportunity being offered at UT."[4] Fred considered the decision to attend UT a compromise. "I chose UT because the sense of change in early 1960 was palpable and I wanted to be a part of it at the largest university in my home state."

When Fred entered UT in 1960, he enrolled in architectural engineering. He thought the engineering degree would give him a more technical background and perhaps prepare him for more job opportunities. But after one semester in architectural engineering, he was convinced to change to the School of Architecture by a friend studying architecture. "These kinds of conversations [among black students] were common," Fred recalls, "and no doubt, in our vacuum of institutional indifference, helped many find their way [at UT]." The attempt to make that transition was thwarted initially by the lack of prerequisites and then by a failure to maintain the grades required to enroll in architecture. After three years of struggle, the cumulative toll of cultural conflict on campus, the political stress of the times, and academic roadblocks in being accepted to the School of Architecture resulted in Fred leaving school.

The cultural climate of the United States was a tumultuous combination of racial tension and political upheaval. That national discourse was represented and articulated loudly on the Forty Acres. What complicated things even more was the duality of challenging the American political system and civil rights while also fighting for a better student experience at UT. Fred, like many of his Black male peers, was not able to cope with the unfair burdens required of them to survive UT. Faced with scholastic probation, he realized his student deferral was at risk. By volunteering for service he would have more choices available rather than risk the draft and be sent to fight in Vietnam. Fred enlisted in the army and served for three years. "Initially drawn to the physical and mental demands of the military, I briefly considered an army career, but a series of scheduling setbacks in pursuing an officer career, along with the buildup in Vietnam, convinced me to return to school at the end of my enlistment," he said. Fred explained:

> In my absence [while in the service] the civil and voting rights legislation of 1964 and 1965 had knocked down barriers to public accommodations and political expression. The now almost total freedom of

movement and choice was welcome, but I still felt consciously wary as though Jim Crow may no longer stalk but might still lurk in hidden pockets of racism and segregation. Surprisingly I found few, causing me to wonder if those last years of segregation in Austin and UT were just a false front propped up by diehards. With rare exception the people I encountered day to day were either just inquisitive or even indifferent about race, were expert at masking their intolerance, or were morphing into undefined, more covert forms of racial prejudice. In the wider view though, race issues permeated African American life.

Fred quickly found work as a draftsman in the architecture firm of William J. Scudder, a Texas A&M alumnus, and returned to school for one ill-fated semester in the fall of 1967. The combination of being a returning veteran, newly married, and older than most other undergraduate students proved to be too much of an adjustment for Fred. He recalls he and Vivian, his wife, visiting Emma Long Park and making the decision that he would work full-time and earn his license through equivalent work credits.

> My only contact with Black students during this time was in the East Austin club scene, particularly one run by Lonnie Fogle for a short time called the Afro Club. There, students felt free to dress in Afro-centric styles and discuss the always-changing local and volatile national Black power scene while listening and dancing to popular R&B, Latin, and African beats.

Fred continued working full-time until 1971 when a reevaluation revealed that the shorter route would be to return to school for a degree. "I reenrolled in 1971 and entered the School of Architecture for the very first time, more than ten years after my first attempt," he said. His academic performance improved greatly, and he completed his degree requirements in the summer session of 1974.

After a two-year apprenticeship, Fred took and passed the licensing exam in 1976. By then Fred felt he and his family needed a change of scenery, so he declined a partnership offer from the local firm where he had been working for nine years and decided to move to Los Angeles. Initially he worked for KDG Architects and Planners, headed by Robert Kennard, a pioneering African American architect in Southern California, and then for Gruen Associates. At Gruen he worked for Norma Sklarek in the production office. Norma was a pioneer as well, being the first Black female licensed architect in the United States. In 1978, missing Texas and not envisioning a long-term future in Los Angeles, Fred accepted an offer to move to Dallas and open an office with two upperclassmen mentors who graduated from UT's School of Architecture in the early 1960s. He headed that office until 1994, when he accepted an offer from UT Southwestern Medical Center to become its university architect. "As important as UT's School of Architecture was to my professional life, the entire university experience transformed my entire perspective on life. The experiences, exposure to ideas, and perspective gained in university during my extended stay gave me base and form. Who I was entering in 1960 was certainly not who left in 1974." Further diving into his reflection on his time at UT, Fred said,

> The UT School of Architecture equipped me with the necessary technical tools for that noble art. Though long in coming that accomplishment was my original and purposeful goal. However, this recollection of experiences lived during those extended years has in comparison of then to now, reinforced a previously held thought; that even after more than fifty years of progress, we as potentially perfectible humans remain somewhere in childhood. For that reason it is secondary in importance only to that original goal that the university experience also provided me with the analytical foundation and life laboratories to look at and live in the resulting sometimes irrational world and make those judgments necessary to live an examined life, one that has ultimately been worth living.

■ HOOVER ALEXANDER

"It's important to build a monument that we were here" was the sentiment shared by Hoover Alexander when reflecting on the legacy of Black students at the University of Texas at Austin.[5] The monument that he alluded to would stand not only as a testament to the lived experiences of Black students on the Forty Acres but a living reminder of the work to be done to remove all impending obstacles to an equitable educational experience for students of color.

A native Austinite, Hoover Alexander grew up in East Austin. His entire childhood took place within the Twelfth Street corridor, attending elementary school and high school in the confined space designated for Black people at the time. The first in his family to be born in a city, Hoover was exposed to resources and experiences never offered to his parents. His family came from rural Utley, a small farm town near Austin. In the 1960s his family sold off the land they owned and moved to the Manchaca area. With exposure to the life lessons that the agricultural lifestyle offered, Hoover's parents believed education would provide their children with the resources to have choices. "Education was really important to my mother and father. My parents worked two jobs for me and my brother to attend private school. I went to My Lady Guadalupe." Hoover was one of a handful of Black kids at the school, as most of the students in the parish were Mexican American. Although most of Austin was segregated at the time, the 1960s offered some instances of interaction. "We had white students from the air force base, then the black Cubanos and Latinos. I have great memories from that time; I learned a lot being around so many cultures." Hoover's maturation in such a diverse community would become pivotal to his collegiate and professional journey.

Although Hoover's private-school background would provide him a unique and privileged experience, it would also complicate his socialization and challenge identity politics. "I lived right at the border of Black and brown and would walk that line on my way home from school, back to the Black part of the city. I stood out in the neighborhood, because we wore uniforms and we went to private school. . . . Walking home with a handful of books, there was a lot of teasing. There was a stereotype of books being equated with being white. It was an interesting dynamic." The quality of education and aspiration to achieve education were often conflated with being white or living in the western part of town. Hoover struggled with the desire to pursue such achievements, while maintaining what his classmates understood as his black identity.

Despite the social teasing that came with private school, Hoover's parents believed that the discipline carried out by the nuns and the high expectations set by the school were a priority. Yet the cost of the school became too burdensome. Hoover and his siblings transferred to Martin Middle School, their local public school. "It was my first experience outside of the integrated cocoon of private school," Hoover recalled. "For the first time I really had to deal with issues concerning race and the gang war amongst Blacks vs. Hispanics." At that time, much of East Austin was split among Mexican Americans and Blacks. The Pachucas, a gang made up of predominantly Mexican Americans, stood guard over the part of East Austin that Hoover frequented on his way to and from school. "They'd take metal bottle caps and put them on the tips of their boots. I have some terrifying memories of walking back with Black friends to get back to the safe zone of Seventh Street . . . to get back to 'where we belonged.'" Carving out a space of belonging would be a lifelong battle for Hoover and most of East Austin's Black youth, particularly in the years following the integration of Austin schools.

During Hoover's first few years of high school, Austin High School offered voluntary integration. That process started with Clarksville and then moved its way into East Austin. "It failed miserably. They cherry-picked white kids to come to East Side schools and Black students to go to Austin High. Most white parents opposed the system." Finally, in 1971 Austin Independent School District closed L. C. Anderson High School, Austin's first and only all-Black high school. Black students were then shuffled to Austin, Lanier, McCallum, Reagan, and Crockett High Schools. "It was not an easy transition," explained Hoover. "We made national news about our riots, which was quite something for the little sleepy town of Austin. It was quite a year." To quell the tension, the school district created a Human Relations Committee led by Hazell Obey and selected white, Black, and Hispanic representatives to coax their peers into cooperation with the integration transition.[6] Hoover recalls that the committee meetings seemed ineffective, yet progress was made. In 1971, Ron Kirk (who eventually became mayor of Dallas and then a US trade representative during the Obama administration) was elected student body president at Reagan High School. "I remember that being such a cool moment to see one of ours in a position like that," Hoover said. Although Austin schools became integrated, the schools soon became socially segregated, with white, rich kids at one school and Black and brown kids filling up others.

The integration taking place at the local level was reflected by, and in some ways informed by, the integration taking place in the state's flagship institution of higher learning, the University of Texas at Austin. When it came time for Hoover to choose a school, most of his family disapproved of his decision to go to UT. "At the same time that [we] were experiencing local tension and making national headlines, the UT football [program] was integrating. Most of my relatives and neighbors had great resentment and hate towards Darrell K. Royal for taking so long to integrate." Despite their hesitation at Hoover matriculating to a school they did not believe truly embodied or believed in values of equality and equity, they "were proud and saluted me for embarking on this journey. There were mixed emotions. It was hard coming from the East Side and knowing what UT represented for folks who lived in that community. My uncles died rooting for UT losses," said Hoover.

Hoover was accepted to UT his junior year, with cost a major factor in his decision to attend. UT was inexpensive, close, and convenient. "I thought to myself, there's a premier college right in my backyard and HT was much more expensive." During his first year, Hoover lived at home and made the ten-minute commute to campus for class. "It helped living at home that first year. There was a lot of support or buy-in from family and community members—I embodied their dreams of what's possible and dreams they never got," he said. The idea of being able to go out and compete in the larger, integrated world was a new reality for the Alexander family and much of the East Austin community. Hoover represented their fears and possibilities. The short trek to the UT campus offered more than an education; it offered potential.

> I didn't have the benefit of having the legacy of college from my parents. So I had to go out and do it how I thought it should be. I wasn't surrounded by people who I could mimic or get coached from. I was trailblazing for lots of folks. I felt I was carrying a lot of hopes and dreams on my back. And then had the negative chatter from growing up with resentment and challenges. But I was arrogant and had the fortitude of "I got this."

While Hoover's time at UT was encouraged by family and friends, it was reinforced by support and intervention of people like Mama Duren and programs like Project Info. Nearly twenty years after the era of integration was ushered in, Mama Duren continued to serve as a nurturing presence for students like Hoover. "She made me feel special. She made us feel like we were valuable members of the UT community," he recalled. As the number of Black students on campus grew, there was a desperate need to replicate what she and other individuals meant to students—mentor, counselor, tutor, and campus mother. Project Info was poised to do just that. Project Info was a minority recruitment organization focused on attracting students from underrepresented populations to consider UT. "That program gave me purpose. I would travel to Dallas, El Paso, and go to inner-city schools and recruit—they paid for our travel and gave us a stipend." Hoover was motivated to make his reality the reality of other kids of color in Texas. "With Project Info, I would go into the inner city and sell UT. But the tough sell was we are only one percent of the population. Social opportunities were self-made."

That same fervor to make UT home to more students of color was the same passion that drove Hoover's investment in creating community on campus. "I was sort of radical. I got really involved and met with a lot of students in Jester. We established relationships early on—my roommates from Silsbee and Sealy. And then the athletes who lived in Jester West, Raymond Clayborn, Alfred Jackson. We found ourselves bonding over racial issues and civil rights." Black students naturally gravitated toward one another for protection, nourishment, and empowerment. The social life of Black students often intersected with civic engagement and social justice efforts. There was no clear demarcation between the cultural expression, political engagement, and social activity. "I don't recall there being an expectation to be included in other things socially. The Blacks partied and generally hung together separately. We generally ate together, played together. People would only branch out out of necessity. Like join the Engineering Club, because it would look good on their résumé, knowing good and well they'd be the only Black person present." This moment in time was contemporaneous to the Black Pride movement, a cultural moment, that Hoover said was strong and salient on the Forty Acres. "There was a sense of 'separate but equal'; we do our own thing, listen to our music."

Many of the students from the larger cities were critical of Austin's lack of social offerings and cultural spaces for Black people. "So we'd frequent Houston and Dallas on the weekends and come back to campus feeling refreshed," he said. Another social outlet for Hoover was the fraternity. While not nearly as robust as their white counterparts, Black fraternities and sororities were present on campus. "I was an Alpha. It was wonderful to have that

type of brotherhood. One of the parties I remember Roosevelt Leaks coming to. We'd throw parties in houses off of Riverside Road, and I would practice my skills as a bartender. A lot of the guys remember me cooking stuff. Jocks like Roosevelt and Jeremy Lamb would come over just because they knew I'd be cooking." The social life manufactured by Black students on campus and in Austin "kept us alive," as Hoover explained.

Hoover was first exposed to the culinary arts through his parents' agricultural background. He understood the work that went into farming and sourcing food. But he owes UT for leading him to a passion for cooking and a future career as a restaurateur and owner of the well-known Hoover's Cooking on Manor Road east of campus.

Only a few years before Hoover entered UT, the restaurants and shops on the Drag were integrated. One of the first establishments to do so was the popular Night Hawk. The restaurant offered Hoo-

The original Night Hawk restaurant located on the Drag. (Austin History Center)

ver one of his first jobs while in college and exposed him to life in the kitchen. "My stepfather was one of the chefs at the Night Hawk, and I applied to work there my second semester at UT. They hired me at the bottom of the food chain. But I had been instilled with the value of taking pride in all that you do. So I took on the job of busboy and dishwasher with pride."

Hoover honed his love and skills for cooking at the Night Hawk and achieved a unique and profound vantage point of life in Austin. While attaining a college degree at one of the most competitive state institutions, Hoover worked side by side with Black and brown cooks who had not matriculated past third or fourth grade. "Mr. Leon Harris, who spent almost forty years at the Night Hawk, hadn't reached the third grade and had limited reading skills, but he could read Bible verses and recipes. He and others like him taught me so much about quality, customer service, and life. I always felt I was the bearer of their hopes, dreams, and what was possible."

Hoover Alexander bartending at the Night Hawk in 1978, a place he credits for helping integrate much of the Drag and developing his skills in the kitchen. (*Austin Chronicle*, April 16, 1999)

While UT had opened its doors to Hoover and his peers, there were generations before him that watched from afar, not able to participate in the equity of a college education. "There was definitely resentment from many of the men I worked with, of UT. A lot of them had been cooks at fraternity houses and sororities on campus. Segregation had limited their access to promotions and well-paying jobs; they were stuck working the servitude jobs. So there was a lot of pride of seeing the young Black students like me come to work and then leave to go to class at UT."

Gymnastics (Open)

L.-R. - Milan M. Kadlecik, All-Around Gymnastics Champion; Charles G. Langham, III, Horizontal Bar Champion; Ronald Rossberg; Trampoline Champion; Robert Frank L'Roy, Parallel Bars Champion, and Side Horse Champion; John M. Lohr, Still Rings Champion; Gary W. Bowman, Long Horse Champion **1962 - 63**

From 1956 until the late 1960s, Black students created their own opportunities for athletic pursuits, forming intramural teams through recreational programs or fraternities. These teams would travel to compete against other Black teams or HBCU teams across the state. Here students pose for their intramural portraits. From a 1956 basketball team and competitive 1957 and 1958 track-and-field teams to a a 1963 gymnastics squad, these were some of the best athletes the campus had to offer. Many were surprised at UT's refusal to utilize the talent available. (The University of Texas at Austin Division of Recreation Sports)

CHAPTER FOUR

Athletes to Unintentional Activists

DURING THE 1950S AND 1960s, a period in American history when the racial landscape was rapidly changing, racial advances in collegiate athletics were taking place across the South. At the University of Texas, that process proved harder to achieve than many expected, as it would take nearly two decades to integrate athletics following the US Supreme Court's ruling that permitted Blacks to attend the university in 1950.[1]

By 1950, UT had established itself as one of the leading Southern universities in both the academic and athletic arenas. Likewise, it began to make headway in addressing the integration quandary, admitting the first Black graduate students to the Forty Acres and being the first university in the South to admit Black undergraduates. "I like the word 'desegregated,' because it certainly wasn't integrated," said Leon Holland, who was an African American freshman in 1956, the first school year UT permitted Black undergraduates. "At that time, nothing was integrated in terms of housing, athletics, bands and extracurricular-type activities."[2]

Driven by the Board of Regents and university leaders who held deep-rooted political and social beliefs against racial integration, the process of total integration was moving slowly, if at all. This attitude toward race would continue into the next decade. In a 1963 article published in the *Daily Texan*, the writer alluded to the regents being responsible for the continued segregation of students in extracurricular activities. "They didn't really integrate," Dwonna Goldstone, author of *Integrating the 40 Acres*, told Grant Abston in an interview, "so, unlike Mississippi that said, 'We don't want them here at all,' Texas said, 'we'll admit them but we're going to segregate them.'"[3]

Two years after a 1961 student referendum called for integration of the university's athletic programs, the UT System Board of Regents removed all of its race-based student restrictions on November 9, 1963. Seven days later, the university's Athletic Council opened its doors to Black athletes for the first time. Nearly a decade after the Southern Conference called for all varsity sports to be integrated, the Texas football program, in efforts to maintain

Julius Whittier during the 1971 football season. Wearing number 67, Whittier stands out in a team photo. (The University of Texas at Austin Athletics)

dominance, opened its recruiting doors to young men of color. The first Black UT Austin varsity football player was Julius Whittier. Having observed the likes of Jerry LeVias at Southern Methodist University and Sam "Bam" Cunningham at the University of Southern California, Darrell Royal put his faith in the San Antonio high school football standout: "I knew he could play for us and handle any difficulties off the field."[4] Yet the significance of his position on the Texas team had little effect on him. "I was a jock, plain and simple," Whittier said. "I didn't care about civil rights or making a mark. I just wanted to play big-time football."[5]

While the gridiron had yet to be officially integrated prior to Whittier's recruitment,[6] smaller, less visible athletic inclusive efforts had been made. After the Supreme Court decision in *Brown v. Board of Education* in 1954, Marion Ford Jr., an aspiring football player, applied to the University of Texas as a transfer student from the University of Illinois and became one of the first seven Black undergraduates ever admitted. Yet in an effort to maintain a segregated university, the regents announced that Black undergraduates "would be admitted only after satisfactory completion of freshmen pre-requisites for their program at a tax-supported and accredited institution of higher education for African Americans in Texas."[7] The university rescinded the admissions of Ford and the other students after Ford publicly stated that along with pursuing his bachelor's degree, he also wanted to play football. His statements challenged the regents' previously implemented policy that barred "participation of Negroes in football games," even though the Long-horns were en route to a 1–9 record, their only victory coming by one point against Tulane. Two days after a demoralizing loss to the Sooners, coach Ed Price was in his office at Gregory Gym when he got a surprise visitor. Ford came in to introduce himself and offer his services. Ford told Price a bit about his background: he had been an all-state lineman at Wheatley High School in Houston, had spent two years at the University of Illinois before transfer-ring to UT, and was in shape. "Ed," Ford said, "you need me. I can help you." Price, who had been head coach for the last five seasons, knew with his cur-rent record he would be fired at the end of the season, but he gave no consid-eration to Marion Ford's proposal. "I just can't do it, son. My hands are tied," were Price's words of woe.[8]

Marion Ford during his high school career, a career that garnered interest from some of the best football programs in the country. (The Dolph Briscoe Center for American History)

On February 29, 1964, nearly a decade after Ford demonstrated his desire to play Longhorn football and a decade after the first Black undergraduates had made their way to campus, UT finally began to integrate the athletic pro-gram, when Oliver Patterson and James Means ran in a track meet in Col-lege Station. But in the struggle to integrate sports at UT, football was always the primary concern. Goldstone writes, "For any home game, tens of thou-sands of white fans filled the Texas Memorial Stadium to watch their white sons and brothers run up and down the gridiron with the pigskin. Many of these whites saw the Texas football team as a bastion of white supremacy that could not be tainted by a black athlete."[9] She writes that administrators and coaches expressed concern about where an integrated team would stay dur-ing travel to away games, since hotels and restaurants across the South were segregated. UT officials, coaches, and supporters unfairly blamed the team's lack of Black players on the poor academics of Black student-athletes.[10]

The situation wasn't much different on Central Texas high school fields. Austin High and L. C. Anderson were recognized as having "the best two teams in the state in the late 1950s," according to Ed Roby, who is an active board member for the Prairie View Interscholastic League Coaches Associa-tion. "They never got to play," he says, "and they were right across town."[11] In those days, L. C. Anderson High School was still the pride of East Austin,[12] and Prairie View Interscholastic League oversaw all of the athletic competi-tions for Black public schools. In addition to its 1942 title, Anderson's football

James Means became the first Black athlete allowed to compete in a Longhorn jersey and to earn a scholarship. The son of Austin activist Bertha Means, James competed on the track-and-field team in 1965. While a talented athlete, he struggled with the "gentlemen's rules" of the South and was sometimes not allowed to stay with the rest of the team and/or compete on certain campuses in the conference. (The Dolph Briscoe Center for American History)

team won the Prairie View Interscholastic League championship in 1956, 1957, and 1961. Austin High, meanwhile, went to the University Interscholastic League playoffs in 1957 for the final time that century, led by quarterback Mike Cotten, who went on to quarterback the University of Texas Longhorns. For most of the twentieth century, schools like Prairie View A&M were the athletic bastions of Texas football for African Americans. Most of the top athletes matriculated to Prairie View and Texas Southern. Despite the demonstrated talent on Anderson's football teams, no Anderson players ever got a chance to suit up for the Longhorns, which remained a segregated team until 1970.

In 1961, the executive board of the Campus Interracial Committee gathered three thousand student signatures supporting athletic integration. The Student Assembly voted 23–0 to petition the regents to adopt a policy supporting athletic integration after they conducted a survey that revealed 74 percent of students favored athletic integration.[13] The General Faculty Council called for the university to pursue integration of all campus activities, and students submitted a petition to the regents containing six thousand signatures in support of athletic integration. UT's student body president also joined six other Southwest Conference (SWC) school student body presidents in signing a resolution promoting integration. Dwonna Goldstone notes the efforts of students and faculty in support of athletic integration that perhaps played a role in the regents' decision. It was a historic ruling for the SWC. Texas became the first SWC program to integrate its athletic programs. Darrell Royal, athletic director at the time, told reporters: "Any bona fide student who is qualified academically and athletically is welcome to try out for any of our athletic programs."[14]

A column in the *Daily Texan* described the social shift best, noting that SWC schools had operated under a "gentlemen's agreement" not to integrate in previous years but recognized the school's political evolution: "We are extremely proud of our Board of Regents for deciding to be men instead of gentlemen. And we are glad to see that they may have instigated a state-wide awakening."[15] The first Black player appeared in a SWC football game in 1966. John Hill Westbrook, a walk-on running back at Baylor University, appeared in a September game against Syracuse. Running back Jerry LeVias was the first Black scholarship athlete in the SWC after signing to play for Southern Methodist University in 1965. After a year on the freshman team, LeVias made his varsity appearance in the first game of the 1966 season and would go on to become an All-American, academic All-American, and the first Black SWC Player of the Year in 1968.

As other SWC schools began to integrate their programs, the University of Texas lagged behind. Even non-SWC member and Texas arch-rival Oklahoma made Prentice Gautt the first Black athlete to receive a scholarship at a major Southern school in 1958. Gautt went on to earn All-Big-Eight football honors twice and was named an academic All-American. Other programs used Texas's racist image to help steer athletes away from Austin. The success of Texas football served as further deterrent to recruit Black players; teams were winning without Black players. Texas had a football team with a record of 60–15–1 and had won two national championships, in 1963 and 1969, since desegregating athletics. Both championship teams were all white. But the 1969 team would be the last all-white team to win an NCAA football championship.

Darrell K. Royal coached the last all-white varsity Longhorn football team in 1969 and helped usher in the first African American recruits in 1970. (The Dolph Briscoe Center for American History)

The 1970s era of Longhorn football challenged both the athletic talents of Black players and their ability to navigate the politicization of their place on the team and campus. In a 1969 *Daily Texan* article, a reporter wrote, "An 80-yard touchdown run by a fleet Negro halfback will do wonders in dissolving racial antipathy."[16]

▪ HENRY "DOC" REEVES

Discussion of the story of integration in the United States often never starts at the beginning. The "firsts," the pioneers, are traditionally and incorrectly associated with the vanguard of the civil rights era, a time rooted in challenging the system. But for many institutions, education or otherwise, the story, although not as visible or bold, starts long before then. Such is true concerning the conversation of race and athletics at the University of Texas at Austin.

In the 1880s in Austin, UT students had begun pressing the administration for a gymnasium. Completed in 1889, the north wing of the Old Main Building, the school's first, included an enormous basement dedicated to storage. Negotiations between students and administration to convert some of this space into a gymnasium were unsuccessful due to funding. In 1896, however, San Antonio banker George Brackenridge offered a donation of six hundred dollars. The school immediately began construction, lowering the basement floor enough to create an eleven-foot ceiling. Lockers and showers occupied one end of the space; students purchased exercise equipment and contributed funds to join the newly formed Athletic Association and gain access to the facility.

The social landscape of Austin in the late 1800s predestined a marginalized experience for African Americans. Concentrated in Clarksville, a community founded by freedman Charles Clark, African Americans had developed a burgeoning livelihood supported by domestic work in the surrounding white communities and at the small, yet influential University of Texas. At the time the college was committed to and facilitated the grooming of young white men for prosperous professional careers and state leadership. The school was much more interested in establishing a respectable academic reputation than investing in extracurricular activities like athletics. Yet the World War I period saw a surge in athletic appreciation from baseball to football, and in the fall semester 1889 the university continued its support of advancing athletics by hiring an instructor, Homer Curtiss, to teach "physical culture," which all male freshmen were required to take, and a facilities janitor, Henry Reeves.

Born in Tennessee in 1872, Reeves was the third of five children of former slaves Benjamin and Sarah Reeves. Sometime between 1880 and 1897 the family moved to Austin. Benjamin found work as a mail carrier. Unusual at the time, Henry had learned to read and write, an advantage as he entered adulthood and looked for work. When Reeves began his employment at UT, the football team was entering its fifth season. His work as a janitor eventually led to his assignment at the gym, in charge of managing the building and keeping it clean, and there he began to engage with the football team. That engagement grew over the years, and soon Henry was functioning as water boy, equipment manager, and assistant to the coaches. As Reeves built trust with the players, he created his own role on the team, earning him the nickname "Doc." The nickname was functional as well as personal, since he often helped injured players off the field, bandaging cuts, wrapping sprained ankles, and doctoring injuries.

Reeves's contributions to the team were widely appreciated by the team and recognized by the UT community. In the campus publication the *Longhorn* in 1914, the paper referred to him as "the most famous character connected with football at University of Texas. . . . He likes the game of football, and loves the boys that play it."[17] He took pride in the work he did, the relationships he built, and the opportunity he had to participate in a game largely unavailable to African Americans. His steadfast commitment to the team and contributions to grooming the players offered a new picture of African American men to UT administrators and the community at large. The team's loyalty to Reeves was tested on numerous occasions, from weekend trips out of town where he was forbidden from riding in the same train car as the team, to an administrator's attempt to dismiss him as an employee. In both cases, the students defended Reeves, confirming his value to the program and to the UT community. Reeves's tenure at the University of Texas spanned almost twenty years of the football team's early history, leaving a lasting mark on the landscape of athletics at UT. Likewise, Reeves set the stage for the integration of athletics, demonstrating a fearlessness of being a pioneer. In the UT yearbook, the *Cactus*, in the early 1900s, editors published a list of the "all-time teams," one of which was "Henry's team."

Henry "Doc" Reeves (The University of Texas at Austin Athletics)

Henry "Doc" Reeves tends to an injured football player on the field. (The University of Texas at Austin Athletics)

Another indicator of his popularity and willingness to lend an ear was shown in the 1908 Rules for Freshmen. Rule number eight was "freshmen shall report diligently to Dr. Henry Reeves for mental ablutions."[18] Henry Reeves died February 19, 1916, at the age of forty-four. He was buried in Austin's Bethany Cemetery, the first burial ground in the city reserved exclusively for Blacks. His passing received mention in newspapers around the state.

■ **ROOSEVELT LEAKS**

In the fall of 1971 Julius Whittier's historic role as the first African American football player on the University of Texas at Austin was overshadowed by a talent lured from Brenham, Texas. In the previous seasons UT had watched schools in Texas and across the Southwest recruit skillful African American athletes to their program; competition like the University of Southern California and Southern Methodist University had players of color tearing up opponents' fields with a speed and strength that caused the Southwest Conference to shift its approach to the sport and social politics. The consequence of Southern schools fighting to remain competitive was integration. Athletes like Roosevelt Leaks became of historic significance on and off the field.

Roosevelt Leaks grew up in rural Texas and attended high school in Brenham. A versatile athlete, he played several sports throughout junior high and high school. He was particularly successful at football and baseball. But at the time football offered the best opportunity for him and many of his contemporaries to attend college. In his junior year he was named an All-American, the same season his team's record was 12–1–1. This type of dominance, while uncontested under the lights of a large football field, would be a predictor of Leaks's career at UT.

When Leaks entered high school, it was the first year of public-sanctioned integration in most of Texas. "My class was the first class to go through integration," Leaks recalled.[19] "They began sending us to the white schools and turned the Black school into a junior high school." This was a trend seen across the South. As high schools began integrating, the question to desegregate athletic programs was inevitable, giving African Americans an opportunity to be scouted and recruited to major Texas colleges. "I got offered opportunities to play almost everywhere, but I couldn't go to Texas A&M because my father told me I couldn't. So the University of Houston was the first school to show interest in me and that I visited." But after visits to the University of Houston and Stanford University, Leaks settled on UT. With UT's great academic reputation and close proximity to his home in Brenham, its contentious history with race on and off the field played a secondary role in Leaks's decision. "It was Prairie View or Texas Southern for most kids that looked like me, but I realized that my grades were pretty decent and I had a talent that could take me to a different type of school, for a different kind of experience. Texas was the best option to have that experience and be close to home. It was important to me to be close enough that my parents could come see me play."

Leaks recalls his introduction to the Forty Acres as surprisingly transparent. "When I went on my recruiting trip to UT, I was hosted by Lonnie Bennett, who was a freshman at the time, and Julius Whittier and Leon O'Neill [who eventually transferred to Southwest Texas, now Texas State], who were both sophomores. The conversations we had weren't particularly inspiring, as they disclosed that they were each navigating some tough waters as the only Black kids on the team and much of campus." But when Roosevelt entered his freshman year, he did not experience the same culture shock as some of his predecessors or contemporary peers of color. "My high school was probably seventy/thirty or seventy-five/twenty-five. It wasn't a culture shock for me to come to UT. Some of the teams I played against in high school, their teams were predominantly white. I played with and against them. There were also several white baseball players from my high school that were going to UT." Accompanying Leaks in his freshman recruiting class was one other Black football player, Fred Perry. Adding some additional support were a couple of Black student-athletes on the track and basketball teams. "There were not a whole lot of Black athletes at the time, so we all hung out together," he said.

Roosevelt Leaks sits on the bench during a game in 1974. (The University of Texas at Austin Athletics)

Leaks learned early on that his experience as an athlete was not like that of other students on campus. "There were definitely perks and doors that were open to me because of my name and my athletic ability that wouldn't have been open to other students of color. I was very much aware of that." Roosevelt's unique experience as a Black athlete and a superstar athlete in some ways isolated him from the challenging social climate and racial tension on campus. Caught between the visceral racism of some of his peers across the Southern region and the more subtle, institutional discrimination of the Forty Acres, Leaks found himself shifting his focus to what he could control—performing on the gridiron.

"I knew several of the Black players on other teams in our conference. One of the players at SMU told me this story of playing for the first time in Dallas. He said students from SMU let loose a whole bunch of black cats on the field in his honor, right before the game started. Some of the things they went through on their campus . . . it was tough. Most of the schools in the South had a similar mentality."

While Coach Darrell Royal had finally come around to recruiting athletes of color with the backing of the athletic administration, opening the door did not instantaneously break tensions in the community or on campus. Reflecting on these earlier decades of integrated athletics, former UT athletic director DeLoss Dodds, who served from 1981 to 2013, said, "The fact there were Black athletes at Texas opened people's eyes. I think athletics in some sense led the way in acceptance and encouraging Black parents to send their kids to Texas. We looked good for the world and it set a standard, a comfort level for the rest of campus." [20] That line of thinking was reflected in the experience of many of the first Black football players.

"We were given the Black recruits to tour, and it was our job to help them feel welcome, comfortable, and make it seem that Texas was the place for them," said Leaks. "But during my sophomore and junior year Texas did not recruit any Black players." Coaches around the region who were competing for the same recruits would often tell potential players of color that they would ride the bench at Texas and that they were better off socially at another school. Both of those years were standout years for Leaks on the field. He was the team's leading rusher during his sophomore and junior years.

Roosevelt Leaks
displaying his Hall
of Fame running
back skills. (The
University of Texas
at Austin Athletics)

On November 4, 1973, he smashed the Southwest Conference record for rushing. According to the *Houston Chronicle*, "Ragin' Rosey ripped off a 53-yard touchdown run, which not only set a new conference record at 342 yards, but fell just eight yards shy of the then-NCAA record set by Eric Allen of Michigan State."[21] Leaks's teammate Lonnie Bennett said, "Leaks has provided the image of a black superstar for us. . . . In five years, it will make a big difference. That's what he's done for blacks here."[22]

In Leaks's final year in a Longhorn jersey, he was injured during spring training, had surgery, and suffered from injuries all season. That year UT recruited its largest class of African American players, including Don Ealy and Howard Shaw, both Tyler Junior College transfers, along with Lionel Johnson, Ivy Suber, Pat Kennedy, and Raymond Clayborn in the spring of 1973. The largest class was the spring of 1974 with Earl Campbell leading that class. This particular group of Black athletes would change UT football and the UT landscape forever.

But attending the University of Texas was never just about football for Roosevelt Leaks; it meant something to challenge himself in the classroom as well. He knew how fortunate he was to attend college, particularly a school like UT, and was dedicated to taking advantage of his opportunity. His aspirations, however, were temporarily dampened when he struggled in the first year and was placed on academic probation. "I really had to learn how to learn. The classes moved at a fast pace, and I had to learn to ask for help and focus. I had some great help though; UT truly offered me great resources."

Those resources included a tutor that helped teach Leaks the techniques and skills to excel in his classes. "My tutor's name was Bill Lyons, and he happened to be one of the only Black tutors on campus. I remember that Bill was everywhere; he was one busy guy, because not only was he smart, but he was well respected and trusted by the other Black students and particularly student-athletes."

Bill Lyons was just one of the many unexpected friendships that Leaks developed while at UT. Like many of Leaks's predecessors and peers across the country who were helping break the color barriers in the athletic arena, the ability to navigate relational tensions was both an art form and a requirement for being a "first." "I was definitely expected to uphold a certain image and be a peacemaker. It took a certain mentality to come to UT and get along with my teammates." Leaks recalls early on some of his teammates messing with him about the role he was often forced to play but reflects that that role of bridge builder continues to inform his approach to life. "I learned a lot having to navigate this strange and at times hostile world, but a true testament to it all is that I'm still friends with my white teammates till this day. There is still great comradery with both white and Black teammates from my playing days. What we started at UT on the football field is a lifelong understanding and friendship."

As history shows, Leaks was not the first Black athlete at UT nor was he the first to play on the gridiron, but his presence on campus and his accomplishments on the field demonstrated the turning tide. His accomplishments managed to garner attention from white Texas, while signaling to Black athletes they could make it at UT. In 2005, Leaks was inducted into the College Football Hall of Fame. At the ceremony in New York, the now former Longhorn football coach Mack Brown shared a sentiment that represented Leaks's Longhorn career: "Roosevelt, this university will never be able to thank you enough for having the courage to do what you did. There is no greater disease in this country than racism. We've come a long way since you played, but there is still much to do."[23]

■ RETHA SWINDELL

The narrative surrounding the intersection of sports and race historically focuses on the advancements made by male collegiate and professional athletes. From national treasures like Jesse Owens and Jackie Robinson to lauded activist athletes like Jim Brown and Muhammad Ali, their stories transcend athletics; they embody the story of race, policy, and sports culture in America. It is true that women's athletic programs were quite delayed in development and national recognition, but the stories and experiences of women of color provide a unique and vital thread to the larger context of integration in higher education. This is particularly true in the case of the University of Texas at Austin.

UT's athletic history displays the power of sports to accelerate the social adaptation of integration and racial diversity. Yet UT and many of its then Southwest Conference peers were extremely slow to invite the talents of Black and brown athletes to compete. The development of women's sports programs coincided with the later part of integration of popular male sports. The first athletic scholarship was not offered to a female athlete at UT until 1974. Women were thus faced with the complex task of navigating both the uncharted waters of racial integration and gender social politics. Sports as a pathway to educational opportunity and social mobility for women of color was less defined yet just as transformative. The experience of Retha Swindell, UT's first Black female athlete, who played basketball for Texas from 1975 to 1979, provides a look into an underexplored experience. In a 1990 *Daily*

University Interscholastic League   ·   Fourth Annual
Girls' Track and Field Meet
May 1, 2, 3, 1975
Sponsored and Organized Under the Supervision of
THE BUREAU OF PUBLIC SCHOOL SERVICE
Division of Extension   :   The University of Texas at Austin
Memorial Stadium, Austin, Texas

Official Program 50 cents

Retha Swindell was a multi-star athlete, having played basketball and run track in high school. She wished to pursue both sports in college and attempted to do so her freshman year. Despite winning the triple jump during a few competitions, she was not allowed to compete in the conference meet, having missed several meets because of her obligations during basketball season. (Retha Swindell private collection)

Texan article, Swindell summed up her time at UT and perhaps the experience of many women of color who came after her: "We had big problems. UT was just not seen as a welcoming place for communities of color. It hit morale and recruiting hard. University and administration really needed to reach out and show that they cared."[24]

Retha Swindell was born in North Texas; neither her grandparents nor parents pursued higher education, but it was expected that she would do so. The same aspiration was instilled in Retha and her siblings to achieve athletically. Although Retha's identity was genetically predetermined, as a scholar-athlete, it was frequently disrupted by the political and social landscape of small-town Texas. During her sixth-grade year schools began to integrate, but Black students were given the choice to stay put or make their way to the "good schools." At the appeal of her parents she stayed put until the end of junior high, when all schools became integrated, a transition that would prepare her for the next stage of her educational and athletic journey.

All of Retha's brothers attended Prairie View A&M University. "UT was just another university," Retha said. "I didn't know the significance of being a part of the UT family. My coach didn't even give me the other letters I had. There was a junior college up the road, Panola Junior College. I told UT that Panola said I could play ball and run track; I was so naïve, thinking that was a good deal." But Retha was fortunate to have teachers who provided direction. When she went to visit the UT Austin campus, she recalls it seeming huge. "But I wasn't intimidated," she said. "Once I got there, you have your places that make it smaller. Even though the number of people in my dorm was bigger than the town I grew up in."

At the time Retha was admitted to UT Austin, the campus was nominally integrated. The ban on Black students playing varsity sports was officially lifted in 1963, but there was still considerable resistance to the integration of the school's athletic programs. Julius Whittier became the first African American to letter in a varsity sport at Texas, but not until 1970. The only Black player on the Longhorn football roster, Whittier struggled to find a teammate who would room with him and was ostracized by many of his teammates. But he opened the door to talented students of color not only in football but also in other sports. Larry Robinson and Bill Lyons helped break the color barrier on the men's varsity basketball team in 1968, a few years before Darrell K. Royal recruited the first Black scholar to compete on the gridiron.

This definitive experience would follow Retha to the University of Texas. The heroism of Black males, encouraged by teachers, mentors, and coaches, in their pursuit to end oppression on the playing field and society at large helped advance education and equity for African Americans. The gender parity between female athletes and male athletes, regardless of race, was ever present during Retha's ascension to college prestige. "In high school we were always told we had to be better than our white counterparts," she explained. "We were always taught you have to work, work, work. I remember Bill Russell and Oscar Robertson. I remember watching that group on TV. I remember liking Johnny Roberts from Nebraska; I definitely knew Jesse Owens, and there was definitely pride in seeing them compete. You always wanted to see someone Black on TV. Those male trailblazers represented progress and opportunity for all Black Americans. There was little visible precedent for women of color; our path was less defined and less lauded."

That was the type of environment that female athletes faced. Black women were confronted with the challenge of advocating for more resources for female athletes while also pursuing more social opportunities and administrative support for all Black students. Before the introduction of Title IX, the UT women's basketball team would hold bake sales and car washes to raise funds to travel to games and/or cut expenses by camping out in sleeping bags in the gym of the team they were playing.

The year Retha came to UT Austin, the women's basketball team transitioned from an intramural sport to a varsity sport, thanks to Title IX, which was signed into law in 1972. Coach Rodney Page had been hired to teach physical education in 1972 by Dr. Betty Thompson, who oversaw recreational sports. In the fall of 1973, she asked him to coach the women's basketball team.[25] He was the first Black coach in an official capacity at UT. Page told Texas Athletics writer Natalie England, "I can't say that there was much overt opposition, but at that time in the history of The University of Texas, there were no black head coaches and very few black faculty."[26]

For Retha, Coach Page's position helped make possible her positive experience in a nominally integrated sports environment. "Rodney drove the van to our out-of-town games, washed uniforms, and helped us mature as young women. He made sure we all knew each other. We learned to appreciate everybody's differences. He would even pick whom we roomed with when we traveled. That was important so we didn't form cliques, particularly for me as I was the only Black person on the team." Ultimately, Retha described her team as "unified because we were women"; in essence, there "wasn't enough room to talk about race."

> I pretty much went to class and did what I needed to do. I kept to myself. Retrospectively, perhaps it was out of self-preservation. At any rate, I didn't feel much of any of the hostility of white peers. I knew some African American classmates did; mostly the guys did. It's tougher on them. I can't tell you why, but it was. Some guys didn't finish. It seems like there were more girls than guys that moved on, that made it out of college. When we had our reunion, the girls outnumbered the guys.

But the comfort that came with being a female athlete did not shield Retha from the vulnerability of being Black. She realized that the Black male student athletes were not immune to the kind of discriminatory treatment that other Black men received. Retha was very cognizant of the challenges that Black male athletes faced, despite athletic prowess or campus popularity. "Even I saw Earl Campbell and players of his caliber have to watch their step. I may not have experienced that type of attention or success, but I just knew it was harder for them. They pretty much ruled the dorms, and every girl wanted to date them." But there was a difference in being a Black UT student-athlete on Saturdays and being a Black UT student on Monday morning and every day off campus. "There are things you go through as a Black man that are like no other. Many of our Black brothers came from a family where you are loved and trust people. You have to remind them how they may be seen. But you just have to remind them that they are Black. That is a legitimate conversation. Make them aware, if you are ever stopped, what to do. Just be aware that you could be profiled."

Retha Swindell stands with Coach Jody Conradt hoisting the 1976 NCAA Women's Basketball championship trophy. Conradt was integral to ushering in racial and gender equity in UT athletics. (The University of Texas at Austin Athletics)

When Donna Lopiano was hired as the women's athletic director in 1975, she made it her goal to have "every Longhorn women's team in the top 10 and at least one national title within five years."[27] Reportedly, many wanted Lopiano to fail. One of her first moves was to hire UT Arlington coach Jody Conradt as the UT Austin women's basketball coach, controversial at the time because the team under Coach Page finished the season 21–7. It was also a move, according to writer Lee Michaelson, others besides Page's players found distressing. Michaelson wrote, "While firing the school's only African-American coach, and one who had invested so much of himself in developing the women's basketball program, seemed, at the very least insensitive to racial overtones. It was natural for her to want to put her own person in the job with so much at stake."[28] Michaelson says, however, that Retha, who had been recruited by Page, decided to give Conradt "the benefit of the doubt."[29] In fact, Jody Conradt recalled in a 2007 *Texas Monthly* interview that only two team members decided to stay on the team after Coach Page was fired—Retha and Cathy Self.[30]

Retha would go on to become team captain her final year and would become her team's first All-American. She also holds the Longhorn record for number of rebounds—1,750.

"When journalists, historians, and students ask me about what the experience of being the first Black female basketball player at UT means, it's always puzzling because although I was aware that was my story, my circumstances were just a part of the journey to get me to college and to get me a life beyond my childhood," Retha reflected. "I did what I had to do, and I'm grateful if it has made a difference."

Swindell, the first black female athlete to receive a scholarship at UT, sits with teammates in her final season as a Longhorn. Swindell helped take women in sports at UT beyond racial identity. (UT Athletics)

CHAPTER FIVE

The Social Politics of Gender on the Forty Acres

THE INTERSECTION OF RACE AND GENDER has not been well explored or developed, particularly when retracing the historical narrative of integration and the civil rights movement. In the larger context of the pursuit of racial equality in the United States, the role of women and their unique struggles are not as defined or lauded as those of Black men. To dismiss the intersection of race and gender is problematic. Many Black women in the era of integration were not afforded the luxury of simultaneously championing a seat at the table as a woman and challenging racial prejudice. Sacrifices were made. Black women, who were among the vanguard of racial integration at colleges and universities in Texas and across the South, were confronted with both resisting the system and retaining their perceived feminine roles and responsibilities. Dr. Dorothy Height of the National Council of Negro Women (NCNW) once said that "there was an all-consuming focus on race. We women were expected to put all our energies into it. . . . There was a low tolerance level for . . . questions about women's participation. Because the women asked gender-related questions, men often felt that women were sidetracking the movement's focus on race. It was thought that we were making a lot of fuss about an insignificant issue, that we did not recognize that the [movement] was about racism, not sexism."[1]

Within local communities, Black women served as chief sources for the mobilization of people; without such roles, the movement would not have been as efficient. Understanding the value of Black women to the movement, Height and other women recognized the need for Black female heightened representation and visibility. This broader dynamic and friction also played out on the UT campus, albeit with more subtlety. In documenting the untold stories of UT's first Black women, it becomes clear that many of their social struggles were leveraged to win victories for all Black students. From dorm policies to classroom professor etiquette, Black women's voices became vital to the progression of integration. Black women helped make visible both racist, as well as sexist, practices in the classroom, informing changes in so-cial behavior. Their presence also helped create community, a space where Black students were protected, encouraged, and understood. The Almetris Co-op was a critical part of helping make that transition for Black students in the early days of integration. It was not a dorm or merely off-campus hous-ing; it was a home and a safe haven, reinforced with home cooking, game night, and the motherly guidance of Mama Duren.

While these observations were surely made during the first decades of in-tegration, recognition since then has been slow to come. Even in the forming of the organization now known as the "Precursors," women were not initially considered. The original iteration of the group, "The Dudes," was created by ten Black male alumni. Charles Miles, one of the first to enter UT in that inaugural year for undergraduate integration in 1956, explains the develop-ment of the Precursors: "There were about ten or so of us that really stayed in touch, and we thought we should try and gather a bigger group of us that ex-perienced those first years of integration. It didn't even occur to us until later to include the ladies . . . but we realized eventually that they were a vital part of our experience and maybe we should invite them." Adding with a chuckle, he concluded, "So then of course we had to change the name."[2] Although eventually reconciled, the failure to recognize the Black female experience provides some insight into the institutional challenges for Black women. Black women at UT, students and staff alike, were vital to the story of inte-gration. Their experiences are both intrinsic to and set apart from the greater narrative of race and racial politics at the University of Texas at Austin.

■ ALMETRIS "MAMA" DUREN

Almetris Marsh Duren was teaching home economics at Huston-Tillotson College when she got a call from the University of Texas asking if she would accept a position as housemother at the dormitory being opened for Black women attending UT. It was 1956, and UT had just confirmed it would now admit Black undergraduates. The only dormitory that would be made avail-able to Black women was Eliza Dee Hall, a house owned by Huston-Tillotson and located many blocks from the UT campus. Duren, sensing the signifi-cance of this turn in history, answered the call.

To appease trustees, parents, and community leaders, UT agreed not to offer any on-campus housing for Black students. Parents and trustees wor-ried about the dangers and social implications of white and Black students rooming together. This meant securing housing accommodations beyond the

Forty Acres for the arriving Black undergraduates. Eliza Dee Hall, located in East Austin and operated by the Women's Society of Christian Service of the Methodist Church for young women attending Samuel Huston College, was made available for a limited number of female students in the fall of 1954.[3]

Almetris Duren accepted the offer to take over the Eliza Dee Hall home and would soon affectionately become not just a dorm director but a substitute mother, counselor, mentor, and guardian of Black students. Mama Duren, as she was soon called by almost everyone who met her, recognized immediately that her girls were both physically isolated from the college experience and, more significantly, socially sequestered. To help them overcome their isolation, she welcomed all students, men as well as women, giving them a place to gather, hold social functions, and meet with her for counsel and encouragement. The co-op ultimately became a safe haven for most Black students on campus, supplementing their college experience with a sense of security, familiarity, and a level of investment in their well-being unavailable to them in their campus experience. The added pressures of social exclusion, and in some cases academic underachievement, to the normal hardships of adolescence proved to be an insurmountable challenge for many of the students. Mama Duren took it upon herself to develop a broad network of resources to meet each of these challenges. She fought every day to keep "her" students at UT surviving and thriving.

Duren's approach was nurturing yet no-nonsense, as one young man learned when he informed her he was leaving the university and going back home. He explained that he was out of money, had no place to live, and would not be able to complete the summer session that would enable him to enter UT in good standing in the fall. "No place to live," she asked? "What about Fred or Clayton or Billy?" She quickly got on the phone, calling around until someone offered the student a temporary place to live. "No money?" Duren quipped. "What about work? Any kind of part-time job will do until you get a fellowship." Then, "Have you called your momma yet? Good, then you don't have to because you're not going home; you're staying right here. Now go off to class. You don't want to get behind in your schoolwork."[4] The young man left, as others had before him, a bit overwhelmed but also reassured that he would be able to continue his education. For students who were struggling with their course work, Duren would find other students to tutor them. For the many who were lonely or homesick or uncomfortable on a predominantly white campus, she would talk to them to convince them that they were smart and remind them that they deserved to be there.

Duren was also a source of encouragement for graduate students. According to Dr. Exalton Delco, the only Black graduate student in zoology, there

Women housed in the Whitis Co-op gather for annual photos in the foyer of the dorm (1950s). Mama Duren became both dorm mom and mentor to many of UT's first Black co-eds. (The Dolph Briscoe Center for American History, Almetris Mama Duren Private Collection)

was little to no university support for Black students pursuing hard science studies like physics, chemistry, or botany. "Mama Duren would seek us students out," Delco recalls, "and would bring us in and talk to us, try and quiet us down a bit and give us the support we needed. Were it not for Mrs. Duren," he continued," I'm telling you, you would not have some of the PhDs we have now in chemistry, that I know of personally."[5]

For almost twenty-five years Almetris Duren was the primary housemother-counselor-supporter of virtually all African American students attending the University of Texas. She had a broad network of resources to dispense, and she knew how to galvanize students and get things done in the university community. If she did not know the answers, she knew whom to ask. She worked quietly and without fanfare; she spoke softly but firmly, and students listened to her. Wilhelmina Delco, the first African American elected to the Austin School Board, credits Duren with keeping almost every Black student in college dur-

ing those first years. "She never raised her voice," Delco said, "but she'd tell them 'you're going to stay here and graduate.' She networked—she had an incredible network—she talked, and she had a positive effect on everyone. She kept everybody going. UT owes her a tremendous debt of gratitude."[6]

When Eliza Dee Hall was demolished because it blocked the construction of the new Interstate 35 highway, Duren moved with her girls to a house on Whitis Street, which they immediately named Almetris Co-op. Ten years later, when that dormitory was torn down for the new UT Communications Building, she moved across campus to the Dean of Students Office, where she worked as a counselor and adviser for minority students until her retirement more than a decade later. In her later years Mama Duren lived at Jester Hall on campus, where she continued helping students. It was there, when a group of Black students was standing around the piano singing one evening, that she conceived the idea of and helped create the Innervisions of Blackness

Women from both all-Black female off-campus co-ops celebrate Thanksgiving together, most likely coordinated by Mama Duren. (The Dolph Briscoe Center for American History, Almetris Mama Duren Private Collection)

Choir, still active today. She also started Project Info, UT's first program established to attract minority students to campus.

Mama Duren's work did not go unrewarded. She received the Margaret C. Berry Award for outstanding contributions to student life at the University of Texas, the Presidential Citation for Outstanding Service, the Distinguished Service Award from the Southwest Association of College and University Housing Officers in 1980, and the Nowotny Medal for extraordinary contributions to student life at UT. Mama Duren was the continuing link between Blacks and whites at the university throughout those difficult years. Her ability to mediate between the UT administration, faculty, community politics, and needs of the African American students was an invaluable contribution to the integration process at UT and around the city. There is no greater example of her role as liaison than that of the sit-in of 1964.

As UT ushered in the 1960s, Black students remained in segregated housing. In 1959 "the housing issue mushroomed," according to Almetris Duren and Louise Iscoe.[7] The *Daily Texan* ran an article about the substandard housing for Black students, and that many more Black women needed housing than was available at Whitis Co-op and Almetris Co-op. A student governance committee upheld complaints of students who lived in Whitis Co-op that it was unsafe. The committee reported, "Whitis [Co-op] exemplifies the fact that housing established under the separate but equal rule does not assure that the original establishment or its maintenance will approach or match any 'equal' standard."[8] By 1961 students frequently gathered at the Almetris Co-op to discuss discriminatory practices and ways to resist and challenge the on-campus housing policies that forbade Black students to be in residence halls without written consent from a white peer. They were also not allowed to use the residence hall dining services, water fountains, or piano or loiter in the lobby. Mama Duren, of course, resented the policies and continued to counteract the social tensions by creating community and cultural reinforcement.[9]

In April of that year the Student Assembly adopted a resolution calling for integration of dormitories and even presented proposals for gradual integration. The General Faculty as well voted overwhelmingly in favor of a resolution to end housing segregation. One weekend more than forty Black students entered Kinsolving Dormitory without consent and occupied the lobby for more than an hour, playing the piano and cards until security was called. The next day every Black student on campus was mailed a letter that put them all on notice and requested their presence in the dean's office. After a week of interviews with all Black students to discover who had led the "sit-in," Mama Duren was summoned to meet with the president, chancellor, and dean in hopes that she would aid administration in disciplining the

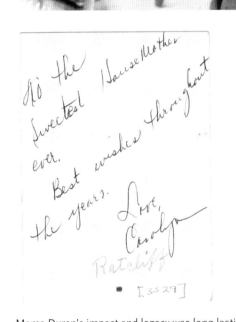
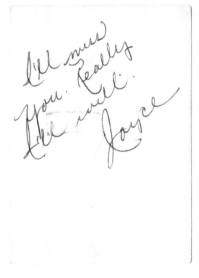

Mama Duren's impact and legacy was long-lasting, and for years she received letters and photos from students thanking her for her role in seeing them through college. The back of these family photos are inscribed with life updates from former students. The first reads "To the sweetest house mother ever. Best wishes throughout the year." The second reads, "I'll miss you. Really, I will." (The Dolph Briscoe Center for American History, Almetris Mama Duren Private Collection)

students. But true to her nature and role as protector and liaison, Mama Duren refused to incriminate any of the students, and none of them were sus-
pended.[10] The students were forever indebted to her love, care, and investment in their future.

■ MAUDIE ATES FOGLE AND SHERRYL GRIFFIN BOZEMAN

"On May 15, 1964, the Board of Regents voted six to one to completely
integrate all university facilities, including dormitories, the following fall,"
wrote Dwonna Goldstone in *Integrating the 40 Acres*. "The regents' actions
made the University of Texas the first school in the South to integrate from
"classroom to dormitory, from stadium to faculty, from band hall to scholarship awards."[13] Three years before the regents' decision, Sherryl Griffin Bozeman and Maudie Ates Fogle lived in Whitis Co-op, one of the few housing options for African American women at the time. The two women were
plaintiffs in a lawsuit filed against the university on November 8, 1961, to
protest the segregation of its dormitories and other campus facilities. But before making their way to the Forty Acres, Bozeman and Fogle were friends
at Evan E. Worthing High School in Houston. The young women enjoyed a
strong bond in high school and shared similar motivating factors in choosing the University of Texas. Against her counselor's advice to attend one of
the HBCU schools in the country, Bozeman chose UT: "I wanted to em-
brace diversity and take advantage of the recent integration," she explained.
Maudie, who would go on to pursue a degree in nursing, had a full scholarship and an array of school options. She ultimately chose UT, recognizing
how significant it would be to attend the state's flagship institution as one of
few Black students.

The young women stepped into unfamiliar territory when they arrived
in Austin. Although they were products of a segregated city and subjected
to racism, nothing had quite prepared them for the social and political climate of the university. Maudie met her future husband, Lonnie Fogle, during freshman year and was introduced to the world of protest and resistance
right away. "I never did that in high school, but when I got here, I got kind
of excited," Maudie once said. "Lonnie and everyone were strong believers in
the power of protest, and I joined in."[14] In 1958, the *Daily Texan* ran a story
about the segregated and clearly substandard living conditions for students
of color. That article became one of the catalysts for students demanding
change. After months of protest, the Grievance Committee undertook an in-
vestigation into the conditions of the Black housing accommodations, which
prompted the university to invest thirty thousand dollars to significantly improve the Whitis Co-op. But cosmetic changes to the dorms were not enough

to quell the protests or the frustration of Black students. Most Black students were forced to live in cramped housing and cope with the difficulties of living off-campus.

The first incident at then-new Kinsolving Dormitory occurred in April 1960. Two Black women were turned away from the cafeteria serving line, although they were invited guests of four white women and had meal vouchers. They were asked to peacefully leave the premises, and although they cooperated at that moment, they expressed their anger to a larger group of Black students later that day. Thus began an earnest effort to integrate the residence halls. That fall, after Maudie and Sherryl arrived on campus, a meeting was called to discuss the future of Black residential life at UT. "We decided to test what would happen if we went back to [Kinsolving]," Maudie recalls. A few days later, Maudie and Sherryl were among a few students who visited Kinsolving to "test" what would happen. Later that evening, all the Black students went to the Kinsolving Dormitory. "We played the piano in the lobby, drank from the water fountain, and just parked ourselves in the center of the dorm. After a little while, security came," said Maudie.

The students dispersed and went back to their segregated residences, but the next day, all Black students on campus were called into the dean's office and asked if they had participated. The dean advised the students to cease the protests or face disciplinary action. Fearful of suspension or expulsion, "we received counsel as to what we could and couldn't say," Maudie said. The protest was covered in the *Daily Texan* and soon was a topic of discussion around the city of Austin and the state of Texas. The issue would not be resolved quietly or easily. When asked why she and others did not back down from challenging the school after the threat of being put on disciplinary probation, Sherryl rebutted, "Because I wanted to finish what was started. I really felt it was not right for us to be segregated."

Sherryl and others not only believed in the ideals of integration but resented being the beneficiaries of a subpar student experience. Black women were forced to live in cramped houses that could not efficiently support more than twenty-five women and endure the complexities of living off campus. After weeks of arguments from all sides of the issue—students, UT administration, chancellors, community members, and elected officials—a lawsuit was filed with Maudie, Sherryl, and a third student, Leroy Sanders, as plaintiffs. The fathers of Maudie and Sherryl were also plaintiffs, and all were represented by the late Sam Houston Clinton, who later became a Texas Court of Appeals judge.

It is critical to recognize that while the lawsuit specifically challenged resident practices and policies by the university, the legal battle would stimulate other policies and much larger conversations and practices. "We were asked if we would be plaintiffs in a class-action suit on behalf of all Black students,"

Maudie said. "There were also some off-campus sites affiliated with UT that were off-limits to Blacks. So our case served as the impetus to do something about a lot more than just [dorms]." The lawsuit did not just affect the girls' lives; it became an issue for their families as well. Their fathers were required to give their consent for their participation, legally involving them in a controversial discussion that did not sit favorably with white people in Austin or Houston. Likewise, the stress of media coverage was overwhelming at times. Maudie's mother was swamped with reporters to the point where she had to stay at a neighbor's house. "I laugh about it now, but it was serious then," Maudie said. There was much to be anxious about, and it was quite a burden for two girls not even out of their teens. "I had mixed feelings through it all," Sherryl remembered. "I didn't know if we would be arrested or verbally assaulted, or if I would be in school the next day, and school meant so much to me. But we had to do something about it." Both considered that avoiding disciplinary action only meant thwarting progress.

In the end, Chancellor Harry Ransom asked Sherryl Griffin Bozeman to withdraw the suit. Out of the three plaintiffs, Sherryl was the only one left on campus. Maudie had married Lonnie Fogle and Leroy had graduated. Bozeman considered her decision carefully. "I knew it was politically expedient for UT to desegregate because the newly installed President of the United States, Lyndon B. Johnson, was coming to serve as commencement speaker at the spring 1964 graduation ceremony, my graduation," she said. She met with Chancellor Ransom in his office and she asked him to put his promise to fully desegregate the university in writing. He agreed, and a while later a messenger delivered a typewritten note from Chancellor Ransom to Sherryl. "It had the tell-tale marks, such as strikeovers, that were signs of a novice typist. I believed that Chancellor Ransom and typed it himself," she wrote in 2010.

Bozeman decided to withdraw the suit. As she recalls, "The University kept its word and we African American students received a victory by the Board of Regents' affirmation on May 15, 1964, days away from my graduation and the day of my birthday."

■ **ANITHA MITCHELL**

Since childhood, Anitha Mitchell had longed to be a doctor. Born in Tyler, Texas, and raised in Dallas, she mapped out her academic trajectory to support her life dream of a medical career. When senior year rolled around, she was all set to attend Howard University, a premier choice for any Black student in 1960 and a popular decision among some of her friends and classmates. But before committing to leave Texas for the Northeast, the Zale Foundation offered her a scholarship, a full four-year ride to the University of Texas at Austin and an additional scholarship to then matriculate to the University of Texas Medical Branch in Galveston. To her parents the choice was obvious and definitive: she would attend UT in the fall of 1961.

Anitha arrived on campus feeling both eager and academically prepared. She had come from James Madison High School in South Dallas, a school known for its exceptional teachers and

One of the off-campus co-ops available to Black female students. (The Dolph Briscoe Center for American History)

what she described as offering "the best free, segregated education" in the country. Not only her school helped set such a solid foundation; she also came from a family of educators. Her father was a high school football coach, and her mother was a second-grade teacher who encouraged Anitha to challenge herself in school and pursue education to its greatest heights. Anitha recalls her mother once saying, "Baby, those white folks don't know any more than you do."[11] Anitha took that to heart and used her mother's words as armor when she walked into a classroom. She would choose a difficult pathway, opting to major in biology, a lonely space for both female and Black students. "I had more problems as a girl than as a Black. In the sciences, that was almost as much of an issue." Anitha, like many of her Black and female peers, encountered ignorant students and prejudiced professors.

Anitha lived on campus in Whitis Co-op from 1961 to 1964. The all-Black, off-campus dorm served as a constant reminder of the Black students' status on campus and that the work needed to be done to fully integrate Black students in the social and cultural fabric of the university. In Anitha's opinion, "If we were going to be students at UT, then we deserved to live on campus and not be segregated."[12] Throughout 1964, she and other students would picket on Sundays at Kinsolving, a large dorm on campus that housed hundreds of white students. While Anitha's strong moral convictions motivated her participation in the protests, she was forced to consider the consequences of her engagement. "I knew that I was in jeopardy of losing my scholarship if I was caught or arrested. So each Sunday after picketing, I would hurry back to our dorm." Home by 6:00 p.m., Anitha made sure her studies did not suffer; she knew how important it was to not let the social challenges of UT deter her from her goal. Looking back on those days, she realized "studying and protesting were my social life."

Then came the summer of 1964. Lyndon B. Johnson was running for president, and his daughter Lynda Johnson lived for a time in Kinsolving Dorm. Mitchell and her fellow picketers prepared a press release to send to the Democratic campaign headquarters, which read, "Your daughter lives in a seg-

Alnita Dunn speaks to other students about advocating for integrated dorms and common spaces in 1958. (Texas Student Publications Collection)

regated dorm." Johnson responded to the letter with urgency and anger and immediately notified the university administration of his support of full desegregation at every level of civil society and, in this case, every level of university life. The reality that his daughter attended a school that enforced a segregated housing policy would have a negative impact on his impending campaign. Spurred by Johnson's political pressure, UT began work to integrate dorm life. A few days after sending the letter, Anitha and several other young Black women got phone calls inviting them to live in Kinsolving. Four of the girls were juniors and were housed together in a suite. Mitchell, a senior, was assigned a room on the first floor, a private room with a bath where she lived alone until her former roommate returned to school for the second semester. Anitha's senior year represented triumph; her voice, sacrifice, and persistence had resulted in a transformative moment for Black students.

Anitha's leadership and community engagement did not go unnoticed. In addition to her work on campus in challenging the university's treatment of Black students, she made time to engage with Black youth in East Austin. She and other students spent time mentoring, tutoring, and engaging students in civil rights dialogue. "It was important for us that these kids and that community saw us Black UT kids on the East Side; it opened up their perspective on their own future." As a result of her exceptional academic standing, leadership, and role in improving life for Black students, she was selected to join the Mortar Board, becoming the first Black woman at UT to become a member of the senior women's honorary organization.

After graduation, Mitchell was wait-listed at Southwestern Medical School but accepted at the University of Texas Medical Branch (UTMB) in Galveston, where she would go on to earn her medical degree. At that time UTMB had more Black students than any other medical school in the country except Howard and Meharry Medical College, both of which were historically Black colleges. After completing an internship at UCLA shortly after medical school, Anitha lived and practiced medicine in the Los Angeles area.

When Anitha left UT in 1964, she, like many of her peers, vowed never to return. Although she had received a quality education, "there were too many unpleasant memories to reconcile." However, at the encouragement of an old friend, she came back to attend the twenty-fifth reunion of her class. To her

Students
protest at a sit-in
in the Kinsolving
dormitory. (Texas
Student Publica-
tions Collection)

surprise, not much had changed. "I ended [up] being the only Black person at the reception, and the bartender questioned my presence there." Reaffirmed in her resentment for the UT experience, she again promised she would not go back to the Forty Acres. But she changed her mind when she got word of the dedication of the Almetris "Mama" Duren Residence Hall. This was too important an event for her to miss; she felt obligated to return for the cere- mony. Duren had not just been her housemother; she was essentially house- mother, mentor, and counselor to all Black students. Anitha recalled Mama Duren's role in her life: "She made campus bearable for me and so many oth- ers." After attending the dedication of the dorm, listening to the tributes, and witnessing all the people whose lives had been enriched by Mama Du- ren, Anitha's heart softened toward the university.

■ **PEGGY HOLLAND**

In the same year UT officially opened its doors to Black undergraduate students, approximately eighty miles south of UT's campus a young Peggy Drake (Holland) was graduating as valedictorian from the segregated Phillis Wheatley High School. At just sixteen years old, she matriculated at her hometown San Antonio College and two years later received an associate of arts degree and was inducted into Phi Theta Kappa (the national junior col- lege honor society). As she transitioned into adulthood, she left home to en- roll at the University of Texas at Austin as a junior in the College of Business. As an only child, leaving her recently widowed mother was of concern, but her desire to attend a "widely recognized university" and her mother's encouragement were incentives for her to come to Austin.

Along with the other Black female students who entered in 1958, Peggy found residence in an old house on Whitis Avenue that had been renovated to meet the needs of twenty-five Black co-eds. On the first floor was a small entry area with a stairway leading to the rooms above, along with living and dining rooms and a large kitchen. Bedrooms, along with a screened-in porch added to accommodate the demand, were upstairs and downstairs. The building, which opened for occupancy in the fall of 1958, was christened Almetris Co-op in honor of housemother Almetris Marsh Duren. Peggy and her peers would come to cherish "Mama" Duren as confidante and counselor, advocate and adviser, and dorm mom.

While Peggy and many of the women in the co-op found comfort in the community they created, experiences on campus and in the classroom were less familiar. When Peggy ventured to the Forty Acres to attend her business classes, she did so alone. "As far as I observed, I was the only African American attending classes in that building until a couple of years later when I saw another African American female going into a classroom." She recalls the students in Waggener Hall avoiding her by choosing seats that were not in close proximity to hers and moving to others if she happened to sit near them. In the hallways, some male students would intentionally bump into her, causing her books and notebooks to fall and scatter about, and she was left out of study groups.

That treatment was not confined to peers. Peggy's experiences with instructors also varied: some positive, some regrettable. "The first of the latter . . . was that of the male teacher with whom I wished to discuss an error in a test grade. I went to his office to discuss the grade. At the entrance to his office, I was told by a staff member that he had 'gone to South America' even as I saw through an open door that he was sitting at his desk." Peggy also recalled a teacher who, on the first day of class, announced that a major part of the grade would be based on class participation when called upon. Peggy's name was never called. Although against the ethical code that institutions of higher learning purport to uphold, these types of slights were nearly impossible to report and even harder to diffuse through policy and administrative oversight. After two years of coping, Peggy decided she needed a breather and a change of scenery and took a job in San Antonio working for the Housing Authority. She returned to UT a year later determined to earn her degree from the College of Business. "I returned to earn a degree in business, because it was my right to be [at UT]."

The unwelcoming and insensitive environment spurred by the mere presence of Black students was somewhat mitigated by moments of friendship

Peggy Drake sits next to fellow Longhorn student and eventual husband Leon Holland
(class of 1960) on campus and at a Longhorn football game with classmate Charles Miles.
(Private collection of Colonel Leon and Mrs. Peggy Holland)

and community. Faculty members who recognized and actively safeguarded the vulnerable Black students were in some ways heroic. During a time when the Ku Klux Klan had a presence in Austin and on campus, Peggy's class had a scheduled trip to Houston for a one-day conference. Students were to ride the bus from campus to Houston and back. When the bus stopped by Peggy's co-op for the morning pickup, her teacher watched from afar as she boarded the bus. The same courtesy was extended on her return. "He showed me both concern and care. He didn't have to be there, but he made his presence felt."

As much as the threat of physical harm tainted the experience of students of color, the intimidation experienced in the classroom was just as harmful. The investment by and guidance of faculty members were invaluable and treasured. "On one hot and humid day, I was walking across campus when a young man hurriedly ran up to me and asked my name. He proceeded to tell me that a professor from whom I had taken a class earlier

Peggy and now
husband Col. Leon
Holland, former
president of the
Precursors, Inc.

wanted to talk to me and requested that I come to his office. When I arrived, the professor asked why I was still in school. I told him I had a grade point problem (actually it was only one point)." His reply was surprising. "He told me that he remembered that I was a good student, as I had taken the report writing class from him and made a good grade. He shared that he believed me to be very intelligent and he knew 'what they were doing.'" That professor then proceeded to advise Peggy to register for a particular class to be taught by a visiting professor from Syracuse University. Peggy followed his advice and did well in the class to qualify for graduation.

In reflecting on her time at UT, Peggy surmised, "My biggest disappointment at the University of Texas at Austin was the attitude of many (but not all) teachers who taught courses in which I was enrolled. Idealist that I was, I innocently and mistakenly assumed that anyone teaching in an institution of higher learning developing young minds would have a different point of view and code of conduct. It is only human to have prejudices, but it is the wise person who knows how not to act upon them. All in all, I recognize that my experiences at the University of Texas served a purpose in preparing me for life, despite the fact that I would not wish many of them upon anyone. Looking back, I feel that the good people I met along the way and other positive encounters outweigh the negatives."

■ BARBARA SMITH CONRAD

Barbara Smith Conrad was born in Atlanta, Texas, the closest city to the town of Center Point, where her parents were teachers at a small rural school. They taught at the first accredited all-Black boarding school in the country. Barbara and her family lived between those two communities throughout her childhood, trekking home to Atlanta on the weekends, summers, and holidays. But Barbara describes growing up in Center Point as "magical." The town was tight-knit and founded by five freed slaves, setting the tone for the community's rich history of Black excellence.

Barbara's mother, Jerrie Lee Cash, set that same tone for her household. "She was an amazing woman, smart, very much the English school marm," Barbara recalls.[15] "We used to call her the sergeant behind her back. She was determined, caring, nurturing. You had to be careful with your language around her. Everybody talked about the fact that she insisted that you be able to speak well, read well, reason well, and that you treated people well. That was important. It was a community." Barbara's father, Conrad Alphonso Smith, brought a heroic fortitude to the family. Born in Leesburg, Texas, he and his brothers all came to Center Point for school with practically nothing. They worked at the school and on the nearby farms to support themselves, where Conrad would eventually meet his wife. They attended Bishop College and pursued careers in education. But not long after Barbara was born, her father went into the military, forging a distinguished career. Born during the Depression, Barbara's mother could not feed and take care

of Barbara and all her siblings, so Barbara would often stay with her most be-
loved great-aunt. Her great-aunt and great-uncle practically raised her until
the age of five. When Barbara returned to her mother and father's house, she
was exposed to and began to develop her love for music. "My brother Dinard
was our child prodigy. He was playing Mozart sonatas at age six, Mama said.
Dinard had the most influence on my early musical development. He went
to Prairie View A&M College." Barbara went to hear Dinard perform with a
male chorus one year in Dallas. They were performing Beethoven's "Mount
of Olives," which is an oratorio piece with a beautiful soprano solo. When he
returned home after the concert, he taught Barbara the song. From then on
Barbara became the family show.

> I remember first singing in Quanah, Texas, because Pappy liked to
> show me off. My aunt Maggie would get me all dressed up in my pin-
> afores, and I would sing in the front yard on a Saturday evening.
> I sang "Yes, Jesus Loves Me" and every little song I knew because
> Pappy wanted me to, dressed up in my beautiful little pinafores made
> by my aunt Maggie from this beautiful fabric from flour sacks. I still
> have one of those dresses.

Center Point Baptist Church became Barbara's platform for musical expression, singing anthems, gospel music, and traditional hymns whenever
the occasion called for it. She was often called on to sing at prayer meetings
and revivals and compete at the Prairie View Interscholastic League (PVIL).
PVIL was the premier athletic and extracurricular competition stage for
Black students around the state. Barbara competed in both the regional and
state competitions and won several times. One of Barbara's teachers, Mrs.
Hatten, recognized Barbara's talent and took her to a radio station in Texarkana to expose her to a wider audience. "I was so nervous that day; I had
never sung on the radio. I hadn't been trained on any special techniques for
singing. I learned by imitation. Because of Dinard and my sister, I grew up
learning the most complicated music not realizing it. Bach, Mozart, Stravin-
sky. I didn't know it was hard. I just sang what I heard."

Barbara's talents were cultivated by her family and supported by her community, creating a safety net for her. But even the wonderful support system
around her could not shield her from the consequences of segregation. Barbara experienced many of the perils of racism through her mother.

> In the same way, I guess segregation bothered me through my mother
> more than directly myself. Having to watch her in Queen City be
> brave and gracious in the face of bigotry. One time, there was a lady

some yards away who was white. She was an excellent dressmaker, and my mother employed her to make some clothes from time to time. To collect them, she had to go to the back door. Going to a department store in Texarkana, not being able to try on a hat because your hair was greasy. "Don't get oil on my hats," they'd say to her. Those were the things that used to absolutely take me from rage to sadness or sadness to rage. The embarrassment, the indignity for my mother, who was smarter than most people I knew. To this day, I go "grrr."

Barbara believed that the counter to such discrimination was "the joy in our lives; there was so much of it."

She explained, "Maybe we had to love each other a little more. Maybe we had to care about each other a little bit more. Maybe we had to try harder to understand our circumstances. Maybe we had to work harder as students to survive and to excel." Taking this mantra to heart, Barbara pursued a career in music with determination. Her heroine, Marian Anderson, drove her passion and purpose to break boundaries. She would begin that journey at Prairie View A&M.

Barbara chose Prairie View A&M University, she said, "because practically everybody in my family had gone there." She had intentions of being a math major but could not ignore her deeply rooted love for music. She committed to music and was nurtured and trained by some wonderful professors and artists. During her second semester, a scout came to campus and heard Barbara sing. He wanted to know her interest in transferring to the University of Texas. After talking it over with her parents, it was decided that she would make the move to Austin to attend UT. They were all in agreement that UT would provide her with greater resources and exposure to support a career in music. Barbara entered UT in 1956, the first year that undergraduate Black students were admitted.

"My first day on campus was a beautiful day. We were an attractive group of young people; perhaps it was because we all thought we were so smart, so bright, and so wonderful. We felt we deserved to be there and walked around as such," said Barbara. But the self-endorsed confidence and empowerment that came from one another and others like Mama Duren were disrupted by the dissent of white students and community members who also greeted them that first day. "As we were walking toward the Main Building, the Tower, there was some jeering. Very little, but it's the one sentence that I wish I could erase from my memory. Some boy screamed out, 'Oh, look at them. Our pappies probably messed around with all of their mammies,' or something like that. My heart stopped and the fury I felt. One of my classmates later recounted that 'you turned purple.'" Barbara and her peers had been drilled to stay silent, to stay dignified and ignore such banter. And for

Barbara Smith Conrad practices the piano in one of the campus recital halls. (The Dolph Briscoe Center for American History)

the most part they were able to do so. During those first few months, that served as an isolated incident, and she carried on with her studies and pursuit of music. "Aside from that, we felt the same excitement and anxiety and all the things that any youngster feels."

Barbara lived in the all-Black Whitis Co-op. Not too far away Black male students resided in an assemblage of old military ROTC barracks. Barbara recalls that living in a segregated residency did not bother her. "We were a great family; I felt connected to my peers, and living with them felt comfortable." Back on campus, Barbara experienced for the most part a supportive environment in the music department, though at times she felt ill prepared. Many of the other students had more experience, motivating Barbara to spend a lot of time practicing in the music building after class.

One day while practicing in one of the music studios, Josephine Antoine (a former Metropolitan Opera diva and a guest lecturer in the UT Music School) barged in and said to Barbara, "My dear, you would be a wonderful Dido." Barbara had no idea what she was referring to, but she accepted Josephine's probing to audition for the opera. The day after the audition, when Barbara entered the classroom, the entire class erupted in applause. Confused by their response and skeptical that their intention was to mock her, she followed her professor's instructions to go look at the bulletin board. "I went to look at the board, and there it was. I had been chosen to perform the lead."

Barbara had won the role of Queen of Carthage. While there was apprehension from her parents and some of her peers about how she would take on this part, Barbara recalls being treated well by others in the cast. "We were just students learning music together and learning how to perform it, learning about staging, and learning about developing characters together." Such support was eventually upset by outside voices and threats. Barbara began to get calls lambasting her casting in the opera and threating to confront her if she continued. "We would occasionally get crank calls; at first it was nothing that made me that nervous. We mostly would pass it off as another sad soul. Then it became a little more ominous, because they would talk about places I had sung. I remember having sung at the Lutheran Church right on campus. They'd say it was not permissible to have a 'nigra' girl sing at this church and I needed to go home, to go back and be with my own. Ugly names. Hard to say them, even today," she recalled.

Barbara relied on the support of the Black community in Austin. "They made us feel that we had a place here. They looked after us. We had someplace to go. That was very important. It was the Black people of Austin and a few white ones who really helped to nurture that part of our lives." Their support would be paramount.

A few weeks into rehearsal and after weeks of enduring degrading calls and letters from people admonishing her for her role in the production, she learned that she would not be allowed to perform in the opera. College of Fine Arts dean Ezra William Doty called Barbara in for a meeting and informed her that the Board of Regents, the president of the university, her house mother, and a few concerned citizens expressed concern for her well-being. "He said that was his least proud moment," Barbara recalled. People were afraid that a major incident would occur at one of her performances, and they were not confident in their ability to stop it. Barbara would be asked to resign from her role in the opera and was warned not to tell anyone except her parents about the decision. It was a painful decision for Barbara:

> You take away something that is that meaningful for a young person, and then you stuff their mouths with cement. I was beyond heartbroken. I lived in a place of heartbreak and rage, rage at a system that could let that happen, from a man I respected and adored. I left that office that day and I was different. I was changed, because if Dean Doty could do that to me, then who could I trust? It took me many years to understand the position he was in.

Barbara Smith Conrad chose to stay at the university and earn her degree. Following graduation, she moved to New York, where, with support from the Harry Belafonte Foundation, she studied drama, dance, and foreign language. Then her music career took off, with performances with the New York City Opera, the Houston Opera, and, in time, throughout Europe. One highlight was portraying her heroine, Marian Anderson, in the TV movie *Eleanor and Franklin: The White House Years*. One of her career highlights came when she auditioned for James Levine at the Metropolitan Opera and was selected to perform. "It doesn't get any higher than that," she said. "Metropolitan Opera was something you dreamed of."

After that, doors opened everywhere. She credited hard work and perseverance, plus talent and opportunity. "Hard work is a big part of it. And not giving up. It's too hard unless it is truly your calling and your passion. It has to be your magnificent obsession. It really does," she said. Barbara, like many of her peers who had also endured the first year of integration, had little interest in returning to the Forty Acres. While their degrees from UT remained a proud accomplishment, their connections

BARBARA CONRAD, Mezzo-Soprano

Barbara Smith Conrad became a renowned operatic mezzo-soprano of international acclaim. (The Dolph Briscoe Center for American History)

to the school were blemished by memories of isolation and disrespect, robbing some of a traditional student experience. "I guess if I have one huge resentment, other than the obvious one, which is racism, it is that I spent so much time trying to survive here that sometimes I couldn't be the student that I wanted to be. We were often frightened, but we always banded together," Barbara recalled.

In 1987, after decades of living and working in New York and Europe, Barbara received an invitation from UT to return to campus. "My manager called me and said, 'You've been invited by the president.'" Barbara had been invited to attend a luncheon at the Littlefield House by President Peter Flawn and his wife. Initially apprehensive and emotional at the thought of making her way back to an earlier moment and place in time, she ultimately felt it would offer her the opportunity to reconcile her feelings and heal. "To come back to campus having been a successful artist and knowing that I was being wooed because of the way my talents had been recognized and lauded around the world, well that felt good."

A copy of Beulah Taylor's Huston-Tillotson transcript from 1961. Huston-Tillotson was responsible for nurturing many of Austin's Black professionals, as well as the thought leadership, throughout the twentieth century. After graduating with her associates, Beulah became an elementary school teacher. (Private collection of Bettye Taylor)

CHAPTER SIX

Rearing a Longhorn Legacy: The Taylor Family

THE STORY OF INTEGRATION at the University of Texas spans decades and is, debatably, ongoing. As we explore the historical narrative in its entirety, it is important to consider both the individual experiences of Black students and institutional memory made up of students, faculty, staff, administration, and the general public. The unique story of the Taylor family not only helps us understand the pivotal groundbreaking years of the early 1960s at UT but offers insights into collective memory. The family's experience at UT spans two decades, two generations, and various vantage points ranging from student to administration. Their family legacy embodies in every way the story of UT.

In 1937 sixteen-year-old Beulah Taylor (formerly Groves) prepared to leave her hometown of Russell, Texas, a small town outside Nacogdoches. She had spent much of her life around the cotton industry, watching people grow, pick, and sell cotton. Sixteen was rather young to venture out on your own, particularly for a young woman and a woman of color, but she had been groomed to make a life for herself outside what Russell had to offer. And the pursuit of higher education was a part of that plan for the determined striver in this family of preachers and teachers. She was excited to start an entirely new life in a city that offered her surroundings much different from those of the community in which she had been nurtured. Her father arranged for her to live with relatives—a while with a cousin and then with her aunt. "We lived in East Austin. She would cook dinner every night, and every Sunday we attended Peaceful St. James Baptist Church together. It was comforting to have family around to look after me as I explored this unknown world," Beulah said.[1]

Her new church home is where she met a family whose eldest son she asked on a Sadie Hawkins Day date and married after obtaining her teaching credentials. Beulah's professional aspirations in the beginning were less driven by passion and purpose than grounded in stark reality and rationality. "At the time the only thing a Black woman could do was be a maid or teach school, and I didn't want to be a maid, so I chose teaching instead." So she pursued a teaching certificate at Samuel Huston College (now Huston-Tillotson University).

Getting a four-year degree was expensive and in her estimation a slow track to getting into the classroom. "I really wanted to start working. I enjoyed being around kids, teaching them about hard work and watching them blossom," she said. Beulah's first job took her back to the countryside in the small town of Bastrop, about thirty miles southeast of Austin. She taught math and reading there for nearly ten years. "I used a lot of songs in my instruction—mostly religious songs. It always felt easier to engage students with a song." While Beulah worked to mold young minds in the classroom, she and her husband became the parents of ten children of their own.

Beulah Taylor (far right) and her husband eventually had ten children. (Private collection of Bettye Taylor)

Inspired by and motivated for her children, Beulah kept her limited credentials current but also decided she needed a bachelor's degree. "I was determined to get my bachelor's. There was more I wanted to do in the field of education, and it was the example I wanted to set for my children," she said.

In 1961 Beulah enrolled at the University of Texas to pursue a degree in elementary education. She would balance the challenges of mothering eight surviving children and going to school, not to mention the social and political turbulence on campus. Although five years had passed since the first class of Black undergrads had stepped foot on the UT campus, there were ongoing tensions among students and with administrators. Campus dorms were still prohibited to Black students, and much of campus and community life outside the classroom was for white students only. "My first year at UT, there were demonstrations on campus. I remember witnessing Black students touring the campus get rocks thrown at them. It wasn't the most inviting environment," Beulah recalled. But Beulah's responsibilities off campus in some ways sheltered her from challenges facing Black students. "I didn't have much trouble. I focused mostly on my studies and had some great professors and mentors that were very supportive." That support came from Dr. Ira Iscoe and Mrs. Maureen Amis, both white faculty members who would build reputations for investing in the well-being and success of Black students.

In May 1963, she and her two teenage daughters graduated on the same weekend. Evelyn graduated from "old" L. C. Anderson High School to become a cosmetologist, and Bettye, from the recently integrated McCallum High School. In the fall of 1963 Bettye would matriculate at UT Aus-

tin, continuing a long tradition of Taylor
Longhorns.

After graduating, Beulah began teaching at St. John Elementary in northeast
Austin. While there, she discovered her
calling. "I ran into so many children with
so many problems, and I decided I could
do better—help them talk their problems
out. So I decided to become a counselor."
Beulah's determination to pursue a degree and career in early childhood education and psychology was reinforced by her
own need for such services. "There were
many times in my life that I or my children could have used the help of a counselor, but those type of resources weren't
just taboo in our community; they were
completely unavailable to us. I wasn't going to allow that to continue."

In 1967 she went back to UT to get
her master's in psychology. That same
year her son John graduated from Reagan
High School and entered UT as a freshman in the School of Business. Her oldest
son, Art, had enrolled at UT with a track

In 1963, Beulah
Taylor graduated
from the University
of Texas at Austin
with a bachelor's
degree in psychol-
ogy. Three years
later, she earned a
master's degree.
(Private collection
of Bettye Taylor)

scholarship a couple of years earlier, running alongside UT's first Black athlete, James Means. Bettye worked full and part-time intermittently during
her student career, completing a bachelor's degree in education in early childhood and psychology by December 1970. But she attended graduate-level
classes in the spring of 1971 to participate in graduation ceremonies in May
before starting a professional career at the US Department of Health, Education, and Welfare.[2]

In the midst of social unrest, in 1970, five members of the Taylor family were enrolled at the University of Texas. It was not only unique; it was
transformative. Two more of the Taylor children subsequently enrolled after graduating from local high schools—Stephen from Reagan matriculated
at UT's School of Engineering, and Sherri from LBJ High School to music
education.

As her children made their way through the UT system as students, Beulah began working at UT in Student Affairs, as a professional counselor in
the West Mall Psychological Center. Her hiring was groundbreaking, not

Overcoming: A History of Black Integration at the University of Texas at Austin

ALMETRIS MARSH DUREN
in association with LOUISE ISCOE

Inscription to Bettye Taylor, 1983, from Almetris "Mama" Duren in her book *Overcoming: A History of Black Integration at the University of Texas at Austin*; and a copy of the Omega Psi Phi Fraternity signature song, the fraternity that all of the Taylor boys pledged. (Private collection of Bettye Taylor)

THE OMEGA PSI PHI FRATERNITY   143

OUR NATIONAL SONG

Omega Dear

W. MERCER COOK   CHARLES R. DREW

1. O - me - ga dear we are thine own. Thou art our
2. To all thy pre - cepts make us true; Live no - bly
3. Through days of joy or years of pain, To serve thee

life, our love, our home, We'll sing thy prais - es far and
as all real men do, Let man - hood be our eter - nal
e'er will be our aim; And when we say our last good -

nigh,   We' love O - me - ga Psi Phi.
shrine;   With faith in God and heart and mind.
bye,   We'll love O - me - ga Psi Phi.

THE NATIONAL SONG
OF THE OMEGA PSI PHI FRATERNITY

ENTERING YEARS OF TAYLOR FAMILY MEMBERS

- ▪ 1961 Beulah earned BA in Education in 1963, Master's in Counseling Psychology in 1969
- ▪ 1963 Bettye earned BA in Early Childhood Education in 1970, attended Law School 1981–83
- ▪ 1965 Art earned BFA in 1972 after lettering in track, following naval service from 1966–69
- ▪ 1967 John earned BBA in 1975 and MBA in 1990, working through it all as a postal employee
- ▪ 1970 Dewey was awarded a full scholarship in architecture but did not complete a degree
- ▪ 1972 Stephen, a Reagan HS National Merit Scholar, started engineering then joined US Navy
- ▪ 1976 Sherri earned a BA in Music Education in 1980 and MA in 1981

only because she was the first Black student to graduate from UT with a master's in psychology but also the first Black counselor to be hired at the flagship campus. Beulah took pride in being the first but also bore great responsibility in what being the first meant. "I was a counselor to all students, but there was something significant about being a Black counselor for students of color. I provided psychological counseling, encouragement, guiding students as they selected their classes. I helped design their lives, and for students of color I had an opportunity to empathize. We had a special connection, because I knew how it felt to balance the responsibilities of school and the realities of UT and America at the time."

Having remarried, Beulah left UT before Sherri arrived, returning to the Austin Independent School District in 1982. She always considered her choices to attend UT and work at UT as necessary. For her it represented opportunity and progression. "We had a lot of family pride in being Longhorns. But it also came down to financial practicality. Huston-Tillotson was my only choice at one time but became more expensive than UT. And being a UT alum and staff member, I thought it would be a great place for my children to experience as well. It was a nice feeling being on campus together as a family. The fact that all my children got to see me persevere and earn my degree and then go on to work at UT and then follow after me was quite special."

The last Taylor child, Sherri entered UT in 1976. Six of the ten Taylor children attended UT. The family's time on the Forty Acres spanned more than twenty years, contributing both as students and staff. In that time the campus climate evolved. "We got to see race relations progress when we were there. It was a gradual thing. In fact, some people may not have noticed. But I did. We did. There were small shifts in the social experience of students. That mattered."

Beaulah Taylor Cooper spent thirty years in retirement as a volunteer with the Austin Retired Teachers Association, which honored her with a memorial scholarship in her name, given twice already, that helps fund graduating high school students who study to becaome educators.

CHAPTER SEVEN

Inside the Ivory Tower: From Students to Stewards

LIKE MANY INSTITUTIONS OF ITS CALIBER, the University of Texas has made a tradition out of hiring and engaging its alumni. Former students trek back to the Forty Acres to continue to contribute to the legacy of academic, research, athletic, political, and social prowess. This tradition, however, was rare and particularly special for students of color. The opportunity to be hired in the classroom and teach outside an HBCU institution not only afforded grand prestige for the alumni but communicated a milestone in UT's political and social standing in the South and America at large. To fully realize the "dream" of integration, student life was not the only experience to transform; this meant intentionality in hiring and leadership. The few Black students who achieved this shift from students to Longhorn thought leaders in the first few decades of integration carried with them not only their job description but the trusteeship of their entire community—the Black presence on campus and in the greater Austin community.

From the classroom, boardroom, and athletic department, Black alum positioned themselves to continue the difficult yet critical work to make UT a more diverse, inclusive, and equitable institution for all its students.

■ **EXALTON DELCO AND NORCELL HAYWOOD**

Segregation was a pervasive social, political, and economic construction that had been established many years before integration became a university-wide consideration. It was so ingrained in the fabric of the city of Austin that even a large university like UT had difficulty overcoming the stringent societal norms that reinforced segregation. UT's first Black graduate students became keenly aware of such obstacles as the Southern mentality manifested in their professor's attitudes, peer relationships, and lifestyle choices. Although UT students recognized that in many ways the university was ahead of other Texas schools in integrating their campuses, UT students were not satisfied.

In a letter to President Logan Wilson, students wrote that although they "recognized that the University of Texas was one of the first universities in the south to admit Negro undergraduate students," they noted that "significant advances in this direction have ceased. Our present concern is for a resumption of this policy of leadership and desegregation in all areas."[1]

Discrimination and isolation continued to be sources of angst for African American graduate students during the formative years of integration. Exalton Delco, who earned a PhD in zoology and went on to a distinguished career at Huston-Tillotson University, noted that "there were the little things."[2] In an interview with the Division of Diversity and Community Engagement in 2010, he talked about the brown-bag lunches that graduate students in his area of study were encouraged to attend. "We would not always meet in the same place, [but] I was never told where the lunch would be." Delco depended on his peers to inform him of the details. "Somehow they would learn where it was, but I never did. . . . I felt that I was excluded purposely." Delco also talked about his family being the only family not invited to an annual Easter egg hunt given for graduate students by the wife of one of the faculty members. But incidents of discrimination were not constrained to social experiences. Delco recalls being both equally puzzled and upset when receiving a lower grade on an exam question than other students although their answers were the same. "Those were the little things."

Dr. Exalton Delco and his wife, Wilhelmina Delco, in the late 1950s. (Private collection of Exalton Delco)

Delco and others learned to handle these situations with personal determination and community support. "Having come from the South in Houston," Delco said, "I was exposed to some of that growing up. You have to look at it and say, 'What is the most important thing?' And for me the most important thing was the degree. So you could do an awful lot to me, but I was looking for the degree."

Delco's isolating experience in the Department of Zoology was a microcosmic demonstration of what many Black students were facing at both graduate and undergraduate levels. As some students noted in the early 1950s, UT was desegregated but it was not integrated. "Oh, there was no support [from UT]," Delco reflected. "The students were just kind of out there. I'm trying to tell you that when those guys were in physics, chemistry, or in botany, I was the only one in zoology I know of; they had a rough time and Mrs. [Almetris] Duren would bring them in and talk to them and quiet them down a bit. . . . If not for Mrs. Duren, I'm telling you, you would not have some of the PhDs we have now in chemistry that I know of, personally." But Mama Duren's motherly support was not a big enough shield from the inevitable social struggles of Longhorn or Austin life.

Delco witnessed both the disengagement of graduate students in 1956 and the agitation of undergraduate Black students. "It was really bad for the grad students, particularly those who came here alone. I had Mrs. Delco and my family to support me, but for others there was little for them to rely on personally." The push for housing for Black students—and soon not just for places to live but for better housing—had become a major concern of both the UT students and the administration. But it was not the only concern. Black UT students wanted more than a classroom education. In addition to better housing on campus, they wanted the same access as white students to the amenities on the Drag, such as attending theaters or shopping for school supplies and clothing—to participate in activities integral to campus life.

Norcell Haywood and friends Robert Norwood, John Hargis, and Marion Ford were among the first seven African Americans who were initially admitted to the University of Texas at Austin in June 1954. Two months later they found themselves having to consider Texas Southern University and Prairie View A&M instead—the only two schools for African Americans in Texas. University of Texas registrar H. Y. McCown had canceled the registration of the students whom he himself had admitted. The students were told they had to take freshman prerequisites for their program at a tax-supported accredited institution for African Americans in Texas.[3]

"There were no other colleges in the state that had our programs, which is why they [UT] had to admit us in 1954," Norcell Haywood said. Hargis and Haywood ultimately attended Prairie View for a year, but on July 8, 1955, the Board of Regents finally opened admission to all students in all fields of study, and Haywood and more than 100 other African Americans were readmitted. It was "an interesting year when I came back," Norcell reflected. "All the facilities around campus were segregated," he said. "In retrospect, there is nothing to justify us making it out of there. There was no school or legal structure to support us."[4]

Along with his grueling twenty-one-hour graduate pursuits, Haywood was in the ROTC program and worked at the Driskill Hotel and as a restaurant valet. These commitments made it difficult for him and the others to do well academically, and socially they struggled for simple civility. Additional stress was created by UT's inadequate living accommodations for Black students. "This was in the fifties, and we didn't have any civil rights laws," Haywood recalled. "Being on this campus was the closest thing to equality that we as Blacks had."

UT students were not alone in pushing for desegregation. It was part of the large civil rights movement taking place across the country and around the city. Huston-Tillotson College provided a much-needed community for many of the students, including experienced faculty and supportive students

to empower UT students to continue their studies and continue their demands of the UT administration. Starting in the late 1950s and increasingly
in the 1960s, protests were taking place throughout the South. Both Blacks
and whites, but particularly young Blacks, were picketing restaurants and
theaters, public swimming pools, and stores. And changes were taking place.
In just one twelve-month period, from the fall of 1960 to the fall of 1961, the
public schools of New Orleans and Atlanta were desegregated, Blacks were
admitted by law into the University of Georgia, lunch counters and other
public facilities were desegregated in Atlanta and Nashville, and the Freedom
Riders made their famous trip through the South in an effort to desegregate
buses and transportation waiting rooms.[5]

The actions of Black graduate and undergraduate students to challenge
systems of discrimination would have little systemwide effects on campus.
While progress would soon be made in dormitory accommodations, graduate students like Delco would continue to fight to experience life without
having to face racial discrimination. "I'll say it again; I was a student at Fisk,
I was a scholar at the University of Michigan . . . but I was a survivor here at
the University of Texas." Delco's sentiments seemed to sum up many of his
peers' experiences in the early years of integration efforts, including those of
Norcell Haywood, whose steadfast desire to acquire advance studies in architecture would make him the second African American to graduate from the
School of Architecture. "We often said this is our university and we're not going to let anyone take that away."

Haywood and Delco both used their experience at UT to direct their professional pursuits and community commitment. Haywood aimed to use his
career as an architect for social change rather than just contribute to wealth
expansion for a small segment of the population. He understood that a Black
architect with the ability to navigate predominantly white spaces provided a
critical voice and position for leadership in the Black community. Haywood
leveraged his position to speak up for his community and allocate resources
to improve equity. "Architecture is a bourgeois industry," he said, "and has
traditionally been considered something of a luxury and closed to the lower
classes. . . . I am not a civil rights person, but I'm an architect who is civil-
minded," Haywood shared some forty years after first stepping on the UT
campus. He established the group Minority Architecture to encourage and
mentor young Black architects and talked about the importance of building in the urban community. Likewise, Delco and his wife, Wilhelmina,
would commit the next half century impacting Austin's social, educational,
and economic landscape for African Americans. Haywood and Delco, along
with their peers, had laid a foundation for action during their years at UT in
graduate school, and the work to shift the appalling practices of social, po-

litical, and economic discrimination both on the Forty Acres and across the city would continue through the civil rights generation soon to emerge in the 1960s.

■ **JOHN ROBINSON**

Like many generations of Black youth, John Robinson received a first-rate education at Phillis Wheatley High School in Houston, Texas. It was one of the largest segregated, all-Black high schools in Texas, yet materials like band uniforms and textbooks were hand-me-downs from white schools. But sub-par resources were outweighed by the quality of teaching at the school. Most if not all of John's teachers had a master's degree or PhD, but more transformative was their push for their students to succeed. "We were not raised to think that we were an inferior community."[6] That cultural ethos set the foundation for John's pathway in education.

John dreamed of attending the University of Texas at Austin after graduating from Wheatley. The school had integrated eight years earlier, and its reputation among Black communities was mixed. While it provided a prestigious, top-tier educational experience, it came at the cost of contentious social challenges. Furthermore, many felt that Black students were ill equipped to succeed at UT. "Everyone was telling me not to go, but my teachers said, 'If you want to go, we'll see that you're ready.'" To get ready meant John would have to complete algebra, foreign languages, and several college preparatory courses in his senior year. John would not only master his college prep courses but score an impressive 1340 on the SAT. His hard work earned him an IBM scholarship to UT, where he planned to major in zoology.

When John began his studies at UT in 1964, he lived in Brackenridge Hall, an all-Black dorm for males. John recalls that Brackenridge and the Almetris Co-op were some of the few spaces where he had encountered other Black faces. "Almetris Duren was the only Black adult we ever saw on campus. She was more than a dorm mom to the girls; she was the anchor." John was often the only Black student in his classes. As few as they were on campus, they were almost nonexistent in the sciences. Despite the isolating effects of being a minority, John strived to make friends. "My parents had taught me that I was no different from anyone else. I may have come from a segregated environment, but my job was to go to school. I told myself, 'I chose this place. I'm going to succeed.'" In 1965, John's sophomore year, dorms were integrated. For the first time in his life, he would live with a white person. He and his roommate quickly became friends. "He took me home to Laredo over one of the breaks, and several years later I was best man at his wedding."

Until 1965, no on-campus housing was open to Black students. These old military barracks became off-campus housing for Black male students. (The Dolph Briscoe Center for American History)

John's relationships would serve him well throughout his undergraduate and graduate experiences.

John graduated from UT in 1968 but stayed on campus to earn a master's degree in psychology. "I had been a freshman adviser, and when I graduated, Dean of Students Jim Ayers hired me as an assistant." That same year, UT sororities were forced to relocate off campus after refusing to sign an agreement to integrate their Greek organizations. On paper UT was integrated, but the expression of such policies was not playing out favorably for Black students in many cases. More than ten years after integrating at the undergraduate level and three years after integrating dorms and athletics, UT was forcing Black students to reconcile indiscriminate practices on all fronts. Regardless of the space Black students occupied, they still faced biased policies. During this time Dean of Students Dorothy Dean offered counsel to John: "She brought me into her office and told me I needed to learn how not to upset white people, because 'you don't understand them.'" John struggled to come to terms with what that meant for him and his role as a postgraduate student and staff assistant. "In those days it was understood that you didn't complain, so I chose to accept others for who they were, people."

Such acceptance of both people and circumstances created a stability and driving force for John throughout his academic and professional journey from undergraduate to graduate school at UT to earning his PhD at the University of Massachusetts at Amherst and then entering the workforce in the competitive medical field, where he was a pioneer. Despite challenging times at UT, John loved being at the University of Texas. "I'm a Texan; I'm a UT grad," he said. "I went there for academic reasons, but I did more than earn two degrees. I made friends; I accomplished a lot. I hope what I did in those early days of integration has inspired others."

John became the first Black psychologist in the US Air Force, serving from 1973 to 1975, and then served as the first Black director of the counseling center at the University of Massachusetts Boston. Since 1992, he has been a professor of psychiatry and surgery at Howard University College of Medicine.

■ BILL LYONS

For many Black youth growing up in America in the mid-twentieth century, athletics provided a pathway to social mobility, but that opportunity was complicated for those growing up south of the Mason-Dixon line. In fact, for those growing up in the Lone Star State, the idea of playing collegiate ball outside an HBCU was unheard of. That trend explains the unparalleled talent at schools like Prairie View A&M, Southern Baptist, and Texas Southern University at the time. It was not just uncommon for Black athletes to play at flagship programs like those at Baylor, SMU, Rice, University of Houston, Texas A&M, and University of Texas; it was public knowledge that such talent was unwanted, freely articulated by coaches and administrations. After *Sweatt v. Painter* and *Brown v. Board of Education*, Black students and students of color were granted access to the educational resources and experience of places like Texas, but the gridiron and basketball court would remain colorless.[7] The legendary UT football coach Darrell K. Royal infamously shared his sentiments about the practice in 1967, saying that "no Negro will ever play for me." Those words resounded as poignant and piercing for a then high school basketball player, William "Bill" Lyons.

Born and raised in Tyler, Texas, Bill Lyons would be among the first of the incredibly gifted athletes of color born and groomed in the small East Texas city. Although athletically skilled, Bill was raised to believe that education was the sure pathway out of East Texas. His father, a graduate of Prairie View A&M, served as principal of Lunbar High School for much of Bill's adolescence (until it integrated), and his mother, a graduate of Wiley College, served as a lifelong educator. His sister became the first Black woman to graduate from Notre Dame and attend graduate school in chemistry. Thus, higher education was an expectation of the family, an achievement believed to offer opportunity, stability, and protection. Bill described that security as "a life of substance for your family that didn't depend on the mood, motivation, or moral code of white people."[8] In an ironic twist, it would be Bill's ability to navigate and adapt to white social culture that would lead him to the Forty Acres.

Social malleability was a survival tactic that Bill acquired early on. His grandmother, a product of rape (a white slave master and a Black slave woman), was a continued reminder of the power of racism. The conversation about and manifestation of white power were not only visceral in the family's history but pervasive in the small town's social landscape. Decisions, policies, and business development were all controlled by a white majority. Bill approached this reality with reverence and skepticism, observing his mother's relationships with white women who wielded their social position and clout. One such woman, Mrs. Arthur Temple, was the wife of the owner of Temple Industries: "They practically ran East Texas, and yet my mother became quite friendly with her, to such a degree that she planted the seed for me to attend the University of Texas." At the time that seemed like a futile endeavor, because Bill was keenly aware of Texas's stance on Black athletes playing varsity sports at the university. Why would he forgo the opportunity to play at the collegiate level? Instead, he set his sights on attending Prairie View, where he was guaranteed the opportunity to play basketball. But even in the midst of making that decision the words of Mrs. Temple resonated. "She once told me that I should consider UT because I had the temperament to deal with white people." That observation would eventually serve as prophecy. After a year at Prairie View, Bill was recruited to UT to assist in building the men's basketball program.

When Bill arrived at UT, coaches and staff observed his familiar rapport with Black and white athletes. He immediately met with Coach Royal to discuss opportunities for Black players to play football and was known by several white athletes who came from East Texas. The relationships Bill cultivated with student-athletes led to the decision to place him in the athletic dorms, becoming the first Black student to live in Moore-Hill Hall, a historically all-white dorm (like most of the dorms at the time). James Street and Bill Bradley, members of the all-white baseball team, served as bodyguards and social mediators. "I had signs posted on my dorm that read 'Nigger lives here,' and often guys would block the shower or burn books outside my room. James and Bill would make sure people didn't get too close or harm me."

As a transfer student, Bill was not eligible to play when he arrived in 1967 and suffered a career-ending injury right before the season began in 1968. But his rapport with students both Black and white would encourage Coach Leon Black to keep Bill around and leverage his relationship with student-athletes to help attract, retain, and mentor athletes of color. In 1968 UT appointed him a resident assistant assigned to athletes. He eventually became a tutor, helping notable UT athletes, including James Means, a member of the track and field team and the first Black athlete to compete at the varsity level at UT; Sam Bradley, a member of the track and basketball team; and Jimmy Blacklock and Larry Robinson, members of the basketball team. Bill's presence and support not only kept these players eligible to play but encouraged them to remain at UT amid the social hardship. "Part of my motivation to work with my peers in this way was my steadfast belief that we deserved the opportunity to succeed at UT. These were our tax dollars. Our parents had paid taxes for so long, we helped build UT; it was time that we not only got to study there but take advantage of all the offerings of the university—that included athletics."

Outside the Forty Acres, Bill's aptitude for advocating and advancing the cause was just as active. Bill and his fellow Black Longhorns would often venture over to the East Side of Austin seeking community and comfort. East Austin churches and Huston-Tillotson provided much of that support and comfort, and the majority of Black community members were supportive, but there were moments of resentment and resistance. "Sometimes you got more racism from the Blacks than the whites," Bill said. "They called us Uncle Toms and thought we thought we were better than them. I would warn the recruits they'd get it from both sides. It was difficult; it was complicated. We'd sometimes have to defend the white man and this racist school, but somebody had to do it. We had to reassure ourselves and the Black community that our presence there was meaningful and important." Although there were moments of friction, Bill and his peers also had the opportunity to join efforts in the Black community to educate and empower.

Larry Jackson, an activist in Austin at the time, organized a chapter of the Black Panther Party. The focus of the Austin chapter was youth empowerment, providing resources such as free breakfast, reading tutorials, and mentorship. On weekends Black students from UT partnered with the Black Panther Party to bus kids from East Austin to campus and feed them free breakfast and expose them to the opportunities in college. "We'd make the university pay for it. They'd eat in the Student Union. In some ways it was our form of resistance. We didn't have a lot of resources or spaces at our disposal, so we took advantage of the things we had," Bill recalled. To that end, in 1968 there was an effort to establish a centralized space for Black students to gather and experience fellowship. That year the "Black room" (now known to students as the Malcom X Lounge) was established. The room became a safe haven for both Black students and faculty alike. Bill believed it essential to creating community for Blacks at UT and convincing recruits that they would have a place on campus.

Bill Lyons was responsible for recruiting some of UT's first and most talented Black athletes, including UT's first All-American, Earl Campbell. (The University of Texas at Austin Athletics)

Bill ultimately was responsible for the presence of the majority of Black student-athletes for the next few decades. "When I came to UT, it felt like there were about forty Black people on the Forty Acres. I made it my business to use athletics as an avenue to bring more Black students to Texas." But that meant more than just bringing players to campus; it meant creating a system that ensured that Black students would thrive on and off the field. Although retention was challenging, it was the recruitment process that proved most difficult, and not for lack of talent. "We had star athletes all over the state and some right in UT's backyard. Austin's Reagan High School won the 1971 state championship, with the majority of its star players being Black. You would have thought we'd jump at the chance to grab them, but instead those players ended up at Tyler Junior College with the hope to transfer. But for the most part they didn't graduate."

Many talented Black athletes fell through the cracks because of a lack of concerted efforts by big-time programs like Texas Tech, Texas A&M, University of Houston, and Texas that did not take the time to visit players and provide them a pathway to their athletic programs and success. Bill became that ambassador, making home visits to players and their parents to sell them on the dream of Texas athletics. Despite his efforts, it was a slow process.

Coach Darrell Royal had the hardest pathway to integration, consistently blocked and criticized by boosters and fans at buckling to the pressure to "brown" the football field. Texas heroes like Barbara Jordan, Willie Nelson, and President Lyndon B. Johnson offered encouragement and pressure to open Texas football to Black athletes. "President Johnson told Coach Royal that integrating football was necessary; it was the last frontier," said Bill. "So I went on that trip to Julius Whittier's house in San Antonio to convince him and Coach Royal that he was the right one to boldly integrate the Texas gridiron."

Bill often reflects on the words of Mrs. Temple and wonders if that played into how he recruited Black players, particularly that first attempt with Julius. "I knew his father was a doctor and that he'd been exposed to the 'white world.' I was hoping UT wouldn't be a shock. He knew he could handle the football part, and I was confident he could simultaneously navigate the politics of being the first." In 1970 Bill was named the assistant athletic director and assistant football coach, solidifying his role in transforming both Texas football and college football. The decision and process to integrate UT football mirrored the changes taking shape in school policy, local leadership, and national rhetoric. Bill recalls the dynamic created in having Black players on the field, Black community members in the stands, and Black leaders arising in Austin. But the social good that came from recruiting players like Julius Whittier did not compensate for or supersede the need to perform and win. "It's all business; it was all money. At the end of the day we had to win. I never got the sense that it was a moral question or issue for folks like Darrell Royal or other UT administrators. I would later discover that sentiment in my work in politics."

Bill continued his work with athletics and football through the mid-1970s before attending UT Law School. Before making the transition, he helped recruit the first Heisman Trophy winner in UT history, the Tyler Rose, Earl Campbell. Prior to Earl's committing to UT, the Minority Achievement Scholarship program was created. Bill and a few of his Black colleagues would trek down to Houston and up to Dallas and offer the top two Black students in each school five thousand dollars a year to come learn at UT. Bill was not just transforming the football field; he was transforming the Forty Acres. But the desire to diversify UT's athletic arena and academic classroom did not outweigh his concern for the students' well-being and success. "I never sugarcoated it; I was very transparent about what was in store for them. I couldn't go half stepping, because people know when you are lying. So I was truthful; it was going to be tough. . . . Somebody had to break the ice," he said. Bill has come to believe that it was not just breaking the ice for programs and policies but for people as well. "For many people it was about pushing past the political pressures of trustees, boosters, and fans and being exposed to the humanity of these young Black men. These were just talented young men with aspirations to play ball and get an education. Beyond the Xs and Os and Ws and Ls, I ultimately believe Coach Royal connected to humanity."

After his time working in athletics at both the staff and administration levels, Bill had ambitions to become chancellor, but he would ultimately go on to practice law throughout Texas.

■ EDWIN DORN

Edwin Dorn was born in Crockett, Texas. His mother died shortly after his birth. His father, a minister, asked Edwin's mother's family to take care of him. Edwin spent his first six years on a farm near Hempstead Texas, with his Aunt Lishia. For much of that time, the house did not have running water or electricity. When it was time for first grade, he moved to Houston to live with his aunt "Sis" to take advantage of the city schools. While the schools were segregated, Houston at least had the infrastructure and resources to support the school system. "I spent first grade through twelfth grade living in Houston. That meant spending nine months of the year in Houston and the summers back on the farm."[9] That level of sacrifice was indicative of the family's belief in the importance of education and its place in pursuing a better quality of life. Most of Edwin's mother's generation had not matriculated beyond the eighth grade. With a steady support system in place, Edwin was expected to finish high school and pursue a college degree. While living in Houston, Edwin lived in the Third Ward and attended Blackshear Elementary and Jack Yates Senior High School. Houston did not begin the slow-moving process of desegregation until the late 1950s.

> I did quite well in school and got good grades. My two older sisters
> had gone to college but had dropped out. So the hope was that I'd
> go to college and finish. It's important to remember that in the mid-
> twentieth century, college was still a privilege of the elite. Regardless
> of color, higher education was not a feasible pursuit for most of Amer-
> ica. College meant access to another level of opportunity, jobs, and
> life, reserved for the elite or extraordinary. I was offered a scholarship
> to Howard and Fisk, but I chose to come to UT. Even with the schol-
> arship assistance, Howard would have been more expensive than UT.
> It was really a decision based around economics. After I was admitted,
> I wrote a check for ninety-three dollars to cover tuition for my first
> semester.

The discourse around economic feasibility is pivotal to the historical narrative of higher education integration, particularly for those in the South. The
tuition, cost of living, and proximity of a place like the University of Texas
outweighed the social difficulties of attending a newly integrated, majority-
white institution. "Beyond the cost I also wanted to get out of Houston; I
didn't want to go to the University of Houston or Texas Southern and at the
time Rice was still segregated. I wanted to get out of town."

Edwin made the two-and-a-half-hour drive north to Austin without his
family, but not alone. Three of his high school classmates enrolled at UT
with him: French Stone, Keith Maxie, and Ollie Harris. The three friends
roomed together in the same dormitory. "When I was in high school, I was
not aware of how slow UT was to desegregate," recalled Edwin. The comfort
of familiar faces near him helped cushion the reality of a new and unfriendly
environment. "I didn't really know much about it until I arrived at the university. What I knew was that the university had begun desegregation almost
a decade earlier, so I guess I thought they'd be further along than they were."

When Edwin arrived, dorms were still segregated, but that ended up being less of an issue, since he was able to room with his friends from home.
But the ongoing segregation of living and athletics spaces was just proof of
lack of institutional progress. "The first year I was [at UT] there were demonstrations against the continued segregation of the dormitories and varsity
athletics. I participated in some of the demonstrations, but honestly, my focus was on the classroom. I came here to get a college degree, and I was pretty
determined to do just that." Edwin, along with his Black peers, struggled to

During the 1960s the University of Texas became a microcosm of the larger American cultural and political context. In 1962, Dr. Martin Luther King Jr. visited campus to encourage student activists and community leaders in their efforts to change policy and legislation. (The Dolph Briscoe Center for American History)

participate in and contribute to the improvement of Black life on campus while investing time and energy in their academic success. The two goals were often at odds. The greatest divide on the Forty Acres involved the privilege experienced by white students who did not have the burden of defending their place at the institution. "I was resentful of the continuing segregation at the university and around the university, particularly restaurants and stores near campus. And while I was enthusiastic about the impending Civil Rights Act of 1964, I doubted its immediate impact on my experience at UT," he said.

Edwin entered UT just a few months before President John F. Kennedy was assassinated. The national discourse surrounding civil rights and racial equality permeated every layer of society; higher education was no exception. College students across the nation were distressed about the future of social and racial progress in the aftermath of the shooting. "Many of us Black students thought of JFK as a part of the social enlightenment and thought of Lyndon B. Johnson as a crude white man from the South. It wasn't just the sadness surrounding the assassination of a president; it was also distress over his successor. But LBJ turned out to be a champion for civil rights."

Edwin describes the social life at UT as a game of resilience and resourcefulness. Black students discovered avenues to satisfy their culinary, cultural, and collective needs. "At the time I wasn't a particularly social guy, so the idea that fraternities were segregated didn't bother me. You quickly learned if you were Black in the South where you would be comfortable and where you wouldn't be comfortable. I lived in the dorm and ate at the campus eating facilities." The only times Edwin's routine failed him was on Sundays, when the dining hall was closed. There was one place within walking distance that would serve Black patrons. So on Sundays, Edwin walked to the famous UT Drag to the Night Hawk Restaurant. The restaurant was white owned but became the first restaurant in Austin to desegregate—a landmark moment for UT and Austin at large. "That's just how it was; we found a way to have a fulfilling life, despite the university and city's doing very little to support our existence," explained Edwin. "If you wanted to get a haircut, you'd have to walk a couple of miles to East Austin to a barbershop. And if we wanted to socialize, we went east to HT's campus or met up with the women who lived in the Almetris Duren dorm."[10]

Students drew strength in building community. Moments like the ones experienced at Almetris "Mama" Duren's Co-op rejuvenated Black students suffering from the stresses and prejudice often felt in the classroom. Edwin described his experience with faculty: "The interactions were mixed. Some faculty were friendly and welcoming, but a couple made it a point to make me feel uncomfortable. . . . Finding the way to interject the 'N' word in conversation. I didn't sense hostility from everyone, just from the few who made it known they were not on board with the change."

Edwin bounced around a few majors before landing on government. While he started with chemistry and spent time taking English and journalism classes, he ultimately felt a pull to pursue life in public service. "There were a few faculty members who encouraged me to pursue grad school, professors like Bill Livingston, Jim Roach, Carl Leiden, and Bill Goetzmann." But encouragement and support from faculty were not the only experiences that bolstered confidence and a feeling of belonging for Edwin and other Black students.

"At times I felt academically inferior coming from an all-Black high school into this overwhelmingly white university. I was really nervous about it early on, because that's what we'd been taught; we'd been taught that our school performance and our intellectual capacity were inferior to whites'." But during his first semester Edwin discovered that some of his white classmates were a lot less prepared for college than he was. This realization unveiled an important consequence of segregation in K–12 education. "One of the effects of segregation at the time was a lot of very smart African American men and women who could have been lawyers, engineers, doctors, but didn't have the opportunity to do that, so they wound up as our teachers," said Edwin. Segregated Black schools in Texas were home to some of the best educators in the state. Many of the Black students who integrated UT were the recipients of exceptional, individualized teaching and inspiring mentorship. "By the time we entered UT, we were prepared, we were empowered, and we were committed."

The preparation of teachers and support of leaders on campus were maximized by the support of the federal government. What took place in the United States in the 1960s was a growing faith in the ability of the federal government to solve problems that state governments had refused to solve and to pursue racial justice in a way that many states, particularly states of the old Confederacy, had not. Although the impact was not immediate or comprehensive, the passing of the 1964 Civil Rights Act had direct implications for the state of Texas and the Forty Acres. The trickle-down effect of the law initiated pressure on the UT administration to expedite the process of integrating all of university life. This included residency, extracurricular activities, and access to resources. Outside the institutional changes enforced, there was a degree of resistance and relief that Black students felt. Blacks felt they had the law on their side, and the momentum of the "movement" emboldened them to demand full access to the Forty Acres. "The passing of the Civil Rights Act and what transpired after inspired me to take an interest in government, and it has left me with a lingering suspicion of what state government would do if the federal government stopped pressuring for change."

That lingering suspicion anchored much of Edwin's career. He went to graduate school, earning both a master's and a doctorate degree. After years in Washington, he went back to UT to serve as dean at the LBJ School, named after the man who turned JFK's promises into laws that moved the country toward racial justice. When reflecting on his first years back at UT in the last 1990s, Edwin recalls there being a Black student body president and prominent Black athletes. "But, on the other hand, I was acutely aware, attending events at the Headliner's Club, that I was the only Black person in the room. I was acutely aware that in many meetings at the LBJ School, I was often one of the only African Americans in the room. So there is a long way to go. There are times when you say, 'My God, wasn't this my experience forty years ago? Haven't we moved past this?' In some ways we haven't."

■ HARRIET MURPHY

At a civil rights protest at the University of Texas at Austin in the late 1960s, Harriet Murphy, UT Law School class of 1969, remembered holding a sign stating "Put the Black man in the history books." Murphy, who eventually served on the City of Austin Municipal Court for two decades, has done more than her share toward not only putting Black men in the history books but also putting Black women in the halls of fame.

Harriet grew up in Georgia, went to high school in Atlanta, and earned her bachelor's degree at Spelman College. She recalled Atlanta in the 1950s as a thriving civil rights scene, a city humming with influential figures engaged in the struggle for equality. "There were just great leaders there. These were the people that MLK [Martin Luther King Jr.] associated with. These were the people that had a great influence on him being an activist even in high school," she said. "It was not unusual for Martin Luther King to be the leader that he became, growing up in that kind of environment. And it was not unusual for many others who came through Atlanta to become leaders— not only political leaders but just leaders. It was a tremendous environment to grow up in," Harriet continued.[11] "I just think that I'm fortunate to have grown up in that environment, which has always made me very candid and very outspoken, and with belief in my opinions."

Harriet possessed this innate sense of integrity and conviction even in her youth. She laughs as she recounts the story of riding a bus with two friends as a young girl and stubbornly speaking up against the driver when he tried to bully a Black man into exiting through the back door of the bus instead of the front. After that, Harriet said, the mothers of her friends forbade them from going downtown with her anymore lest she stir up trouble with her outspoken comments. It was with this same spirited strength of purpose that Harriet arrived at the University of Texas Law School in 1966. She had been living in Texas for several years. After working as a public school teacher in Georgia and then earning her master's degree from Atlanta University, she had moved to Texas to teach government at Prairie View A&M University. It was there that she met her first husband, a doctor who lived and practiced in Longview and who was visiting at the university's health clinic. After he and Harriet married and relocated to Longview, she put her passion to work advocating with local political leaders in an effort to raise the percentage of African American voters in her county. Though she had for some time thought about attending law school, not until after her husband passed away did she decide to pursue a law degree. She was accepted at the University of Texas at Austin, and as she puts it, "I rolled into town in my white Cadillac in the summer of sixty-six."

"Lo and behold, I was in for a shock," Harriet said, explaining that upon her arrival she discovered that there were only five other women enrolled in the summer class, and there was only one other African American student, but he promptly graduated. "I really don't remember facing the serious problems of segregation that I had faced in Atlanta," Harriet said of her first few years in Austin. She never had any trouble with discriminatory professors in the Law School, though she did face unique problems as the single African American student in the program. "I was not invited to be a part of a study group, and that is so important for preparing for examinations," she said.

As a student, Harriet recalls encountering a great deal of negativity from members of the African American community in Austin. She was repeatedly told she would never be allowed to graduate from the University of Texas because she was Black; and when she did in fact graduate without a problem, she was told that she would never be allowed to pass the bar. "They really believed that. They knew people—they knew Blacks who had started out here and did not finish, and they knew Blacks who had taken the bar and did not pass. I was getting no encouragement there, so I guess what kept me going was the environment that I grew up in, and I knew that one day things would be different," Harriet said.

Harriet was also involved in civil rights activism on campus. "I did protest while I was here," she said. "At that time there were no Blacks on the football team, and there was an activist on the campus—his name was Larry Jackson—and he had organized students to march every Saturday when there was a home game. We would do this marching, and I would come back to school on Monday and worry about whether somebody recognized me in the line, protesting," she recalled with a laugh. She attributed her determination to continue to fight for equal rights to her upbringing. "Still that background in Atlanta coming forth in my life," she said, "making me remember that I had a part to play, that I must play, in helping to bring about equality for African Americans in this country."

While earning her law degree, Harriet taught at Huston-Tillotson University, where she became head of the Government Department. At one point she invited Thurgood Marshall, at the time the US solicitor general, to speak at Huston-Tillotson when he was coming to Austin to visit Lyndon Baines Johnson. His response by letter—which now hangs on her wall—said that his trip would be too short to accommodate a speaking event but asked if they could arrange to have lunch. Harriet recalled expressing her disbelief over the lack of progress at the University of Texas during her meeting with Marshall. "'You know what, Thurgood,' I said, 'after twenty years of *Sweatt v. Painter*, here I am, the only Black at the Law School. And I said that I would have thought that something would have been different.'"

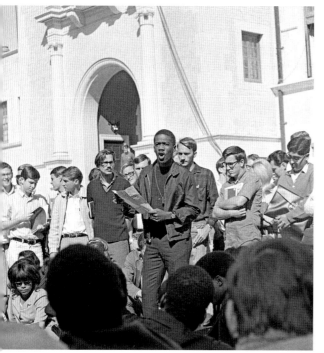

Students protest, challenging the administration to improve the on-campus experience of students of color. (Texas Student Publications Collection)

Because of her perseverance, Harriet has been a great force toward ensuring that things are different in Texas today. In 1973, she became the first African American woman appointed to a regular judgeship in Texas, and she served on the City of Austin Municipal Court for twenty years. She was a charter member of legal and civil rights organizations in Austin, including the Austin Urban League, the Black Lawyers Association, and the Travis County Women Lawyers Association. For her outstanding contributions Harriet has received numerous awards, among them the highest award from the Austin NAACP and the first Thurgood Marshall award bestowed by the students at the UT Law School. She serves on the board of the National Organization of Black Judges, and in 2010 she was inducted into the National Bar Association Hall of Fame.

Harriet remembers how, running into Dr. King once in an airport, King offered her a job with the Southern Christian Leadership Conference. It was right after she had entered law school, Harriet recalled, and her mind was made up that law school was where she wanted to be. "But now I think I would have been more popular if I had been one of his assistants or something," she said with a laugh. Harriet said her life has always been animated by a deep commitment to work toward equality for African Americans, but she became a judge to help all people.

UT Black students protest the status of integration at UT and inequitable experiences for students of color. (Texas Student Publications Collection)

Students register for classes in the 1970s. The late 1970s saw some of the largest numbers of Black students enrolling at UT to date. (The Dolph Briscoe Center for American History)

Students sign a petition to add Black history to the UT curriculum. The table banner reads, "Negro History Course Petition." (The Dolph Briscoe Center for American History)

Members of UT Black-centered clubs and Greek organizations gather for a spring picnic on campus in the late 1970s. (The Dolph Briscoe Center for American History)

Members of Black Greek organizations gather for a joint social function in the 1970s. (The Dolph Briscoe Center for American History, Almetris Mama Duren Private Collection)

Culture Committee sponsors commemoration

"1989 has been a really outstanding year for the Afro-American Culture Committee. Everything we have done has been very well received by the UT community and the community at large," Chairman Christopher Bell, philosophy/government senior, said.

The committee remained active throughout the year providing culture programs, speakers and forums for students and the Austin community. "The purpose of the AACC is to educate and enlighten people about events that are important to our culture," Bell said.

The 30 member committee worked with the community and organized a commemorative march on Jan. 16 for Martin Luther King Jr. Day. To organize the march, members went to churches and black businesses and sent letters to many organizations to gain awareness and support for the march.

"We wanted everybody to participate, not just minorities," Coordinator Lemont Henderson, international business junior, said. "Martin Luther King Jr. didn't just stand for minority issues, he stood for issues for the people."

Over 300 people participated in the march that started at Jester Center and finished at the Huston Tillotson College campus. "It was really nice because it wasn't just black people that came. Blacks, whites, old, young, male and female all participated in the march," Bell said.

On Jan. 17, Martin Luther King Jr. Day, 1350 people attended the third annual celebration sponsored by the committee. The preparation for the reception held in the LBJ auditorium began over the summer. "We had to get police escorts, room reservations, catering, march permits, speakers and contracts," Henderson said. "It was really nice, though. There were people everywhere and there was a special warmth in the air; like one big united family."

According to Bell, "Participating in the march and reception was memorable to me because so many of our parents did things like that, but they did it in a time where segregation was at its highest point. We as students don't have to put up with the over-manifestations of racism that they did, or know the sacrifices they made. In a way, to me, it was my way of saying thanks. You may be gone, but you are certainly not forgotten."

— Denise O'Brien

UNITED TOGETHER: Valeria Milstead, sociology junior, and Gregory Stephens, Austin resident, listen to speakers at the Capitol, Jan. 16. — *photo by George Bridges*

FRONT ROW: Dana Lynn Clack, Sabrina Gail Byerly Claudia Ann Mouton, Emily Kay Burr, April J. Cheatam, LaMetrice Denise Ware, Rachelle LeAnn Young, Paula Yvette Baty, Brandon William Powell. SECOND ROW: Kevin Bernard Crowley, Patsy L. Julius, Kinaya Tanasha Small, Deanna Beverly Dewberry, Markla Vancia Neal-Austin, Deirdre Susan Ricketts, Edward C. Chang, Eric Michael Benjamin, Sharon Denise Watkins. BACK ROW: Kelvin Christopher James, Bertha Alvina Edwards, Deirdre Franchelle Dion Hammons, Christopher DePalm Bell, Sara Lee Jackson, Horacha Elaine Jonus, Joy Lynn Touchstone, Eric Leverte Dixon, James S. Mays, Sidney Lemont Henderson. — *photo by Varden Studios*

AFRO-AMERICAN CULTURE COMMITTEE

In the 1989 *Cactus* yearbook, Denise O'Brien writes about the impact and influence of the Afro-American Culture Committee on campus and beyond. (*Cactus* Yearbook, The University of Texas at Austin)

Black students gather for a social function. (The Dolph Briscoe Center for American History, Almetris Mama Duren Private Collection)

FRONT ROW: Deirdre Franchelle Dion Hammons, Dawn Eustacia Walton, Sonia Catrina Gilmore, Bridget Lanette Braxton, Yvette Chante' Williams. SECOND ROW: Sonya Celeste Mitchell, April Juanita Cheatam, Brandon William Powell, Tracee Dezell Banks, Erica Dawn Shaffer, Paula Renee Handy. THIRD ROW: Markla Vancia Neal-Austin, Norelia Bonetta Reed, Nancy Delia Anderson, Glynniece Anwyl Herron, Sonya LaTraise Pickens. FOURTH ROW: Mayerland Lavon McDonald, Horacha Elaine Jones, Joy Lynn Touchstone, Kevin Bernard Crowley, Sidney Lemont Henderson. FIFTH ROW: Angela Dawn Cook, Shonah Patrice Jefferson, James Avery Bynum, Carlos R. Henderson, Richard William Cook. SIXTH ROW: Gwen Meredith Robison, Tami Coette Parker, Michael William Waugh. BACK ROW: Sonja Reshemah McShan, Eric Leverte Dixon, Larry Mitchell Woodfork, Damon George Munchus, Adam Charles Overton. — photo by Varden Studios

A HAND OF POWER: Zaneta Reed Williams, magazine journalism junior, lifts her arm during an emotional moment of Dr. Yosef Ben Jochannan's speech sponsored by the African-American Culture Committee. — photo by Patrick Humphries

A CALL FOR ACTION AND UNDERSTANDING

On Jan. 15, 1990, more than 3,000 people heard Angela Davis' message.

Davis — author, scholar and human rights activist — was invited to the University by the Texas Union African-American Culture Committee to commemorate the spirit of Martin Luther King, Jr. and his work on the anniversary of his birthday.

Davis' powerful words brought home to many people the problems facing the nation and the role each person had in their solution.

"All of these problems — abortion, poor education, apartheid in South Africa and racism — are all related to people and their basic rights as human beings," Joy Touchstone, Plan II jun-

ior, said.

Keeping to the theme of "Rekindling the Flame: A Renewed Commitment to Activism", Davis strongly conveyed the need for people to continue fighting.

"There are still many problems to be solved and they cannot be solved by themselves," Richard Cook, education senior, said.

"Angela Davis' message to me was the need to continue activism in the black community. The struggle is not over yet for peoples, black or white," Bridget Braxton, communication freshman, said.

Many people came away from Davis' talk with a positive attitude and an overall excitement.

"Several people were fired up. They just wanted to go out and do something," Touchstone said.

Davis' speech concluded an emotional day, which began with a march by students and community members to celebrate King's birthday. The march symbolized the coming together of all Americans, regardless of color, and brought King's dream forward into the 1990s.

"The mission of the African-American Culture Committee is to reach the day when our true African-American history is respected and known on this campus and in the world," Eric Dixon, broadcast journalism junior, said.

The problems facing the black community and other peoples struggling for their basic rights were brought to the forefront by Davis' talk, which renewed activism as well as remembrance of Martin Luther King's work.

The 1990 *Cactus* yearbook recaps the African-American Culture Committee's gathering on January 15, 1990. The event brought together more than five thousand people to commemorate the birthday of Dr. Martin Luther King Jr. with a visit from and a speech by the illustrious Dr. Angela Davis. (*Cactus* Yearbook, The University of Texas at Austin)

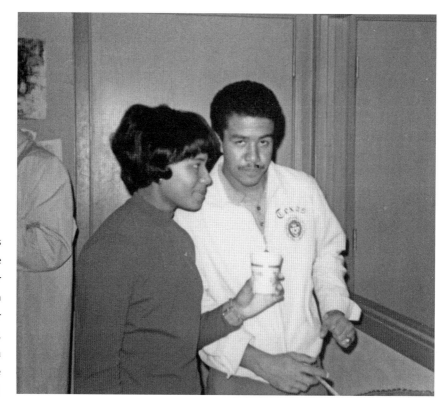

Black students
majoring in the
sciences gather for
a mixer. (The Dolph
Briscoe Center for
American History,
Almetris Mama
Duren Private
Collection)

A former resident of Whitis Co-op sends a photo and note to dorm mother, Almetris "Mama" Duren. The note reads, "To Mrs. Duren, I thank you for all the help you have given me over the years. You have been a great strength to me. Love Shanitta Gale Chism (1974–1977)." (The Dolph Briscoe Center for American History, Almetris Mama Duren Private Collection)

EPILOGUE

Fran Harris

> You may shoot me with your words,
> You may cut me with your eyes,
> You may kill me with your hatefulness,
> But still, like air, I'll rise.
> —MAYA ANGELOU, "STILL I RISE"[1]

THOSE WORDS RANG TRUE from poet Maya Angelou's 1978 poem, but they could also easily be the anthem of African American students enrolling at the University of Texas at Austin in 1956. These students were not only *not* welcomed on the Forty Acres but were also harassed, ridiculed, and in some instances, tortured.

And still, they rose.

Some hailed from the Austin city limits; others, from nearby cities like Houston or Dallas or cities farther away like Fayetteville, Arkansas. With no promises of lavish accommodations or even guarantees of *safe* accommodations for that matter, they enrolled and they arrived.

Now, remember, this was a pre–civil rights era UT. There were no Black professors. No erections of statues on campus of Black men or women who had done great things. No evidence that a Black student could even excel in an all-white public institution like UT. And certainly no signs at the time that they would ever be accepted as full members of UT's exclusive academic society.

And still, they rose.

Armed with confidence, probably a measure of trepidation, and maybe even uncertainty, they set out to prove that education was an inalienable birthright rather than something you earned because you were male, white, or both. They set out to prove that when given the chance, anybody can excel socially and academically. They set out to prove that the stage doesn't need to be set for your success for you to become a shining star. But more than anything they proved that razor-sharp focus and a made-up mind are really all you need to succeed in a world that could care less that you succeed.

Precursor: a person who comes before another of the same kind; a forerunner.

I remember reading a story about Dr. Martin Luther King Jr.'s Montgomery Boycott, where thousands of people would literally walk hundreds of miles in the name of freedom and civil and human rights. One day Dr. King spotted an old woman who had walked several weeks. He was concerned that the toll of walking several days across several cities might be too much for her.

So I can picture him approaching her with a smile, "Mother, you sure you want to do this?" he asked. The old woman probably smiled back with a nod. "Ohhhh, yes sir, Dr. King," I envision her saying. "I'm fine. I can handle this." Today she would say, 'I got this.'"

Dr. King admired the old woman's commitment but likely seemed to feel that it was his duty to let her know that the walks were going to get more brutal even for the youngsters. "Yes, ma'am, but you're old; are you sure you're able to handle the miles?" he asked.

I can see the old woman shooting Dr. King a knowing look as she took a long, deliberate pause and prepared to speak, "My feets is tired but my soul is rested," she's quoted as saying.

VC Players of the Year / Fran Harris, Clarissa Davis, Annette Smith

Fran Harris was a part of the 1986 NCAA National Women's Basketball Championship. She went on to play professionally in the WNBA. (The University of Texas at Austin Athletics)

On another occasion a carpool driver saw another older Black woman barely making it in the rain, so he pulled over, rolled down his window, and said, "Jump in, Grandmother; you don't need to walk."

As the story goes, the old woman just kept on walking and said, "I ain't walking for myself; I'm walking for my chil'ren and my grandchil'ren."

That's what our Precursors did. They walked so we could run. They sat in so we could sit down. They parked out back so we could valet in front. They stood up so we could stand.

I landed on UT's campus in 1982 on a full basketball scholarship.
I had no idea who the Precursors were and what they'd fought for, but I knew *someone* had paid the price for me to be there.

I was born in the West Dallas housing projects. When I was three years old, we moved to Oak Cliff, the southern-central sector of Dallas. I attended predominantly Black elementary, middle, and high schools and had never sat in a classroom of white students except the summer before my senior year at South Oak Cliff High School when, based on an essay contest and several interviews, I won a Gifted Students Institute award to become an exchange student in Cuernavaca, Mexico. That summer of 1981, I was the only Black kid in the traveling party of about thirty. I was aware of my surroundings but almost completely unfazed.

Since I was five or six years old I can remember my mother reminding me that I was just as smart, just as pretty, and just as capable as any other student—Black, white, Latino, Asian, or Native American. "If you don't succeed," she would say, "it ain't because you cain't. It's because you choosin' not to."

She knew I would need those words. And of course, I never forgot those words.

And I would imagine that that's how the Precursors felt that first year at UT and all the years that followed. Students, professors, and administrators might try to make them believe that, they couldn't measure up, but they knew they could. So they kept rising. Instead of breaking them, the racially charged climate at UT actually became an incentive to overcome and succeed at the highest level.

As a student-athlete at the university in the mid-1980s, I had about a half-dozen experiences that served as reminders that, although the Precursors had laid the foundation for a better campus environment, we still had a lot of work to do.

For example, my College of Communication professor told me that "I'd changed his perception of Black athletes." You never know what people are thinking unless they're honest enough to tell you, so those sentiments didn't actually surprise me. My read on him all semester had been that he was waiting on me to do what he believed "we" did when things got tough. Blame the majority for our predicament. Sulk or stand in the background while the white students got all the shine and the accolades.

But I never did. Because Mama's words kept ringing in my ears. "You're as smart as anybody you're ever gonna meet." And so I rose.

The diversity lessons and exclusion experiences didn't stop in the classroom.

I can imagine that the athletes who suited up as Longhorns before I bounced onto campus in 1982 had to endure their share of Precursor-like drama. They often overused the words "natural athlete" to describe those of us who excelled in sports. Somehow it was never that we had put in countless hours of time and practice to achieve excellence or mastery. Our success to them was almost exclusively about our gene pool. Or on the flip side, the

Fran Harris (left) served as moderator for the 2015 Heman Sweat Symposium. The panel included some of UT's first Black female students. Sitting next to her are Judge Harriet Murphy (1969), Judith Jenkins (attended in the 1960s), and Sherryl Griffin Bozeman (1964). (Photo by Shelton Lewis)

overwhelming use of the word "lazy" to describe a Black athlete who didn't quite meet his or her white coach's expectations. Yet a white kid exhibiting the same behaviors or habits wasn't labeled quite as critically.

Even over the span of a twenty-year broadcasting career I have encountered biases from colleagues or producers who seem to think that if I'm not smiling, agreeing, and yessuh bossin' with them every time I see them that they must label me as aloof, uppity, or hard to get to know. I finally had to face the fact that some folks will never be comfortable with a capable, assertive Black woman. I can live with that, and I would imagine our Precursors would bear witness to these kinds of experiences. Yet still we all rise.

I was fortunate to host a magical night with the Precursors in 2015. A night that would validate so much of my experience not only at the University of Texas at Austin but also in the world as a whole. In recognition of the annual Heman Sweatt Symposium, I moderated a panel exploring the politics of race and gender for UT's first black female students. Listening to the panel talk about how determined they were to succeed inspired me beyond words. Reading about them online is one thing. Watching interviews of them on YouTube is another thing. But sitting with them. Touching them. Feeling them. Looking into their eyes and hearing their stories—in their own words—was both empowering and affirming of my own experience.

No doubt their eyes and ears have seen and heard things I can only imagine.

I truly cannot fathom what it took for them to get out of bed in the morning, make a trek to a community of higher learning, and sit in a classroom with an instructor and classmates who don't think you belong there or work in an environment with people who are waiting on you to stumble or fail. Oh, wait . . . yes I can.

And still I rise.

Thank you, to all Precursors—known and unknown—who put their lives on the line so that we could have the opportunities we now enjoy at the University of Texas. Your war scars are not in vain. Not all of the battles have yet been won, but I hope we're making you proud. If it appears sometimes that we aren't fully engaged in the struggles you witnessed firsthand—believe me, we ARE. Most important, though, I hope you know that we appreciate your love and legacy and that, in the words of gospel legend Marvin Sapp, we never would have made it without you.

NOTES

PREFACE

1. Duren and Iscoe, *Overcoming*, x.

INTRODUCTION

1. Goldstone, *Integrating the 40 Acres*; Lavergne, *Before Brown*.
2. The lack of documentation surrounding Black institutional history is quite common. This represents an American phenomenon that mandates intentional efforts such as the development of the National African American History Museum.
3. Duren and Iscoe, *Overcoming*, ix.

CHAPTER ONE

1. Goldstone, *Integrating the 40 Acres*, 15.
2. Gillette, "Blacks Challenge the White University," 321.
3. Frantz, *Forty Acre Follies*, 199–200; Gillette, "Blacks Challenge the White University," 321–22; Goldstone, *Integrating the Forty Acres*, 16.
4. Goldstone, *Integrating the Forty Acres*, 16; Texas House Bill 255, p. 359; Shabazz, *Advancing Democracy*, 30–31.
5. Goldstone, *Integrating the Forty Acres*, 16.
6. Gillette, "Blacks Challenge the White University," 322.
7. Shabazz, *Advancing Democracy*, 31.
8. Frantz, *Forty Acre Follies*, 200.
9. Mettler, "The Only Good Thing Was the G.I. Bill, " 40.
10. Gillette, "Blacks Challenge the White University," 324.
11. Ibid., 324–25; Gillette, "The NAACP in Texas," 41, 50; Lavergne, *Before Brown*, 88–89.
12. Lavergne, "Why Heman Sweatt Still Matters," 79.
13. Sweatt family panel discussion during the Twenty-Fifth Annual Heman Sweatt Symposium on Civil Rights, January 27, 2011, Austin, Texas.
14. Lavergne, *Before Brown*, 89.
15. Ibid., 61, 71.
16. Ibid., 253, 259.

17. Ibid, 286; "The First African American Graduates at the UT School of Law," https://tarlton.law.utexas.edu/african-american-graduates. Virgil C. Lott who had completed one year of law school at Texas State University for Negroes in Houston, also entered law school that year with Sweatt and Washington. He was the first to graduate in 1953.

18. Both the quote from Hemella Sweatt and the story from Heman Sweatt were stated during the Sweatt family panel discussion on January 27, 2011.

19. Ibid.

20. Ibid.

21. Lavergne, "Before Brown," Lecture.

22. Ibid.

23. In 1952, Tillotson College merged with Samuel Huston College to become Huston-Tillotson College. In 1955 it became Huston-Tillotson University.

24. Unless otherwise noted, all quotations in this profile are from W. Astor Kirk's Share Your Story submission, 2011.

25. *Austin American-Statesman*, Dec. 4, 1947, as reported in "Reflections from Applying to Graduate School," by W. Astor Kirk.

26. *Daily Texan*, "Inadequate Negro Schools Caused Move, Says Kirk," December 10, 1947, 1.

27. Weddell, "Library's Ban on Negroes Hits," Part A.

28. Unless otherwise noted, quotations in this profile are from John Chase, interview with Amy Crossette, University Communications staff member, 2008, San Antonio, Texas. Most of the profile is from Crossette, "Following Historic Enrollment."

29. Dolph Briscoe Center for American History, interview with John Chase, October 23, 2006.

30. Ibid.

31. Ibid.

32. Ibid.

33. Kenny and Campbell, "First MA Awarded to Negro Graduate," 1.

34. Briscoe Center for American History, interview with John Chase.

35. Unless otherwise noted, all quotations in this profile are from Doris Askew-Hicks, "The Journey of a 1959 Graduate," unpublished manuscript, submitted for the DDCE's Share Your Story project in 2011.

CHAPTER TWO

1. Gillette, "Blacks Challenge the White University," 338.

2. Lavergne, *Before Brown*, 88–89.

3. Rusch, "One Big 'Cannot,'" 4.

4. Goldstone, *Integrating the Forty Acres*, 73.

5. Austin History Center, "Blue Plate Special."

6. "City Restaurants Sign Integrate Pact," *Austin Statesman*, June 6, 1963.

7. Ibid.

8. Ibid.

9. Frantz, *Forty Acre Follies*, 210.

10. Louise Iscoe, conversation with Helen Spear, 2010.

11. "2 Theaters Integrated for Students," *Austin Statesman*, September 5, 1961.

12. Frantz, *Forty Acre Follies*, 210.

13. Kevin Almasy, interview with Mamie Hans Ewing, March 7, 2017.

14. Kevin Almasy, interview with Walter Chris Jones, November 1, 2016.

15. Kevin Almasy, interview with Mamie Hans Ewing.

16. Kevin Almasy, interview with Emmanual McKinney, November 8, 2016.

17. Kevin Almasy, interview with Mamie Hans Ewing.

18. Ibid.

19. Kevin Almasy, interview with Emmanual McKinney.

20. Louise Iscoe, conversation with Dr. Jerry B. Harvey, 2010. Dr. Harvey was professor emeritus at George Washington University and had been an active member of University Baptist Church. He passed away in 2015.

21. University Baptist Church website, www.ubcaustin.org.

22. "Integrated Schools, Camps, Hines Plea," *Austin American*, January 25, 1958.

23. "Integration Progress Is Praised," *Austin American-Statesman*, June 20, 1963.

24. Announcement of reunion of Human Opportunities Corporation Board, 1982.

25. Hardgrave, "An Academic Odyssey," 199.

26. Duren and Iscoe, *Overcoming*, 8.

CHAPTER THREE

1. Sweatt, "Why I Want to Attend the University of Texas."

2. Unless otherwise noted, all quotations in this profile are from Dorothy Cato's Share Your Story submission.

3. Unless otherwise noted, all quotations are from Rodney Griffin, interview with Jessica Sinn, December 5, 2016.

4. Unless otherwise noted, all quotations in this profile are from Fred Alexander's Share Your Story submission, January 9, 2012.

5. Unless otherwise noted, all quotations in this profile are from Hoover Alexander, interview with Virginia Cumberbatch, August 14, 2014, Austin, Texas.

6. Hazell Falke-Obey was a well-known Austinite active in the NAACP. She worked at Austin High School and then in the offices of Representative Wilhelmina Delco, Governor Mark White, Texas Attorney General Jim Mattox, and Texas Land Commissioner Gary Mauro.

CHAPTER FOUR

1. Ruiz, "UT's First Black Students Faced Significant Discrimination."

2. Abston, "Integrating Texas Athletics," 6.

3. Ibid.

4. Drape, "Changing the Face of Texas Football."

5. Ibid.

6. A Black freshman walk-on player, E. A. Curry had played the previous season during his freshman year but struggled academically and quit. Royal had recruited Leon O'Neal, a Black football, baseball, and basketball player from Killeen in February 1968, but O'Neal quit after a year.

7. Goldstone, *Integrating the Forty Acres*, 115–16.

8. Ibid., 119.

9. Ibid., 120.

10. Ibid., 113, 120–24.

11. Virginia Cumberbatch, personal conversation with Ed Roby, January 2015, Austin, Texas.

12. L. C. Anderson on Thompson Street in East Austin was closed in 1971 to comply with a federal judge's desegregation order. AISD opened another L. C. Anderson High School in the predominantly white Northwest Hills neighborhood in 1973, changing the school colors and mascot.

13. Goldstone, *Integrating the Forty Acres*, 124.

14. Ibid., 126.

15. "Royal Says Negro Athletes Welcome," *Dallas Morning News*, November 19, 1963.

16. Abston, "Integrating Texas Athletics," 12.

17. Little, "Integrating Athletics at the University of Texas at Austin."

18. Nicar, "Rules for Freshmen in 1908."

19. Unless otherwise noted, all quotations in this profile are from Roosevelt Leaks, interview with Virginia Cumberbatch, August 5, 2014, Austin, Texas.

20. DeLoss Dodds, interview with Virginia Cumberbatch, July 19, 2014, Austin, Texas.

21. Callahan, "Longhorns Forgotten Day."

22. Ibid.

23. "Bill Little Commentary: The Pilgrimage."

24. Unless otherwise noted, all quotations are from Retha Swindell, from interview with Virginia Cumberbatch, January 7, 2015, Austin, Texas.

25. "In His Words: Rodney Page Reflects and Remembers."

26. Ibid.

27. Michaelson, "Title IX."

28. Ibid.

29. Ibid.

30. Smith, "Jody Conradt on Retirement."

CHAPTER FIVE

1. Joseph, "Black Women in the Civil Rights Movement."

2. Charles Miles, Precursor celebration, September 9, 2016, University of Texas at Austin.

3. Duren and Iscoe, *Overcoming*, 6.

4. Ibid., ix.

5. Louise Iscoe, interview with Exalton and Wilhelmina Delco, summer 2010.

6. Ibid.

7. Duren and Iscoe, *Overcoming*, 7.

8. Ibid.

9. Cato, Share Your Story submission.

10. Reminiscences of the Precursors, Precursors' annual meeting, Crowne Plaza Hotel, September 11, 2016.

11. Unless otherwise noted, all quotations in this profile are from Anitha Mitchell's Share Your Story submission.

12. Ibid.

13. Goldstone, *Integrating the 40 Acres*, 109–10.

14. All quotations in this profile from Maudie Ates Fogle are from a discussion at the Precursors' annual meeting, September 11, 2016, at the Crowne Plaza Hotel, Austin, Texas. All quotations from Sherryl Griffin Bozeman are from an interview with Virginia Cumberbatch, February 4, 2015.

15. Unless otherwise noted, all quotations in this profile are from the Shirley Bird Perry University of Texas Oral History Project interview, Dolph Briscoe Center for American History.

CHAPTER SIX

1. Quotations in this chapter are taken from Beulah Taylor, interview with Virginia Cumberbatch, May, 13, 2015, Austin, Texas.

2. Education was made a separate department in 1979 and HEW was renamed Health and Human Services.

CHAPTER SEVEN

1. Duren and Iscoe, *Overcoming*, 8.

2. Unless otherwise noted, all quotations are from Exalton Delco, interview with Louise Iscoe, summer 2010.

3. Goldstone, *Integrating the Forty Acres*, 38.

4. All quotations from Norcell Haywood are from an interview with Christopher Palmer, University Communications, and DDCE staff members, summer 2010.

5. Trillin, "Back on the Bus."

6. All quotations from John Robinson are from telephone interview with Louise Iscoe, 2011.

7. Thompson, "Whittier Led the Integration of Texas Football Team."

8. All quotations from Bill Lyons are from interview with Virginia Cumberbatch, January 23, 2015.

9. All quotations from Edwin Dorn are from interview with Virginia Cumberbatch, September 3, 2014.

10. All quotations from Harriet Murphy are from an interview with Christopher Palmer, University Communications, and Meg Halpin, summer 2010, Townes Hall, University of Texas Law School.

EPILOGUE

1. "Still I Rise" from *And Still I Rise: A Book of Poems* by Maya Angelou, copyright © 1978 by Maya Angelou. Used by permission of Random House, an imprint and division of Penguin Random House LLC. All rights reserved.

BIBLIOGRAPHY

Abston, Grant David. "Integrating Texas Athletics: The Forgotten Story of the First Black Basketball Players." Master's thesis, University of Texas at Austin, 2011.

Austin History Center. "Blue Plate Special." Exhibit, 2011.

"Bill Little Commentary: The Pilgrimage." UT Football, December 7, 2005. http://www.texassports.com/news/2005/12/7/120705aad_317.aspx

Callahan, Michael. "Longhorns Forgotten Day: Roosevelt Leaks' Groundbreaking 1973 Game." *Houston Chronicle*, November 4, 2015. http://www.chron.com/sports/longhorns/article/Longhorns-Forgotten-Day-Roosevelt-Leaks-6610260.php.

Crossette, Amy. "Following Historic Enrollment, African American Architect John Saunders Chase Lays Foundation of Firsts." *UT News*, February 4, 2008. https://news.utexas.edu/2008/02/04/chase.

Drape, Joe. "Changing the Face of Texas Football." *New York Times*, December 23, 2005. http://www.nytimes.com/2005/12/23/sports/ncaafootball/changing-the-face-of-texas-football.html?_r=0.

Duren, Almetris M., and Louise Iscoe. *Overcoming: A History of Black Integration at the University of Texas at Austin*. Austin: University of Texas Press, 1979.

"Facing the Winds of Change with Dignity, Courage and Wisdom." Precursors panel discussion, September 9, 2016, LBJ Auditorium, University of Texas at Austin.

Frantz, Joe B. *The Forty Acre Follies*. Austin: Texas Monthly Press, 1983.

Gillette, Michael L. "Blacks Challenge the White University." *Southwestern Historical Quarterly* 86 (July 1995): 321–44.

———. "The NAACP in Texas, 1937–1957." PhD diss., University of Texas at Austin, 1984.

Goldstone, Dwonna. *Integrating the 40 Acres: The Fifty-Year Struggle for Racial Equality at the University of Texas*. Athens: University of Georgia Press, 2012.

Hardgrave, Robert L., Jr. "An Academic Odyssey: West Texas to South India." In *Burnt Orange Britannia*, edited by William Roger Louis. London: I. B. Tauris, 2005.

Hatfield, Edward. "Desegregation of Higher Education." *New Georgia Encyclopedia*, August 2, 2016. http://www.georgiaencyclopedia.org/articles/history-archaeology/desegregation-higher-education.

Holley, Joe. "A Native Texan: A Journey to Law School Integration." *Houston Chronicle*, September 24, 2016.

"In His Words: Rodney Page Reflects and Remembers." UT Women's Basketball, March 1, 2016. http://www.texassports.com/news/2016/3/1/womens-basketball -in-his-words-rodney-page-reflects-and-remembers.aspx.

Joseph, Tiffany D. "Black Women in the Civil Rights Movement: 1960–1970." Freedom Now! Accessed August 21, 2017. http://cds.library.brown.edu/projects /FreedomNow/tiffany_joseph_thesis.html.

Kenny, Bob, and Dorothy Campbell. "First MA Awarded to Negro Graduate." *Daily Texan*, February 6, 1952, 1.

Lavergne, Gary M. *Before Brown: Heman Marion Sweatt, Thurgood Marshall, and the Long Road to Justice*. Austin: University of Texas Press, 2011.

————. "Before Brown." Lecture, 25th Heman Sweatt Symposium on Civil Rights, January 27, 2011, University of Texas at Austin.

————. "Why Heman Sweatt Still Matters." *The Alcalde*, September/October 2010.

Little, Bill. "Integrating Athletics at the University of Texas at Austin." *Texas Media Relations*, February 27, 2014.

Mettler, Suzanne. "The Only Good Thing Was the G.I. Bill: Effects of the Education and Training Provisions on African-American Veterans' Political Participation." *Studies in American Political Development* 19, no. 1 (April 2005): 31–52. doi:10.1017/S0898588X05000027.

Michaelson, Lee. "Title IX: Former Texas Longhorn Reflects on Era of Change." Full Court, June 23, 2012. http://www.fullcourt.com/lee-michaelson/21403/title -ix-former-texas-longhorn-reflects-era-change.

Nicar, Jim. "Rules for Freshmen in 1908." The UT History Corner, June 12, 2012. https://jimnicar.com/2012/06/12/rules-for-freshmen-in-1908/.

"Retha Swindell." *Daily Texan*, 1990.

Ruiz, Leila. "UT's First Black Students Faced Significant Discrimination on the Long Road to Integration." *Daily Texan*, April 4, 2014. http://www.dailytexan online.com/news/2014/04/04/ut's-first-black-students-faced-significant-discrim ination-on-the-long-road-to.

Rusch, Pat. "One Big 'Cannot'—a Negro Student's Life." *Daily Texan*, December 6, 1960, 4.

Shabazz, Amilcar. *Advancing Democracy: African Americans and the Struggle for Access and Equity in Higher Education in Texas*. Chapel Hill: University of North Carolina Press, 2005.

Smith, Evan. "Jody Conradt on Retirement." *Texas Monthly*, August 2007. http:// www.texasmonthly.com/the-culture/jody-conradt/.

Sweatt Family. Panel discussion at the Twenty-Fifth Annual Heman Sweatt Symposium on Civil Rights, January 27, 2011, University of Texas at Austin.

Sweatt, Heman Marion, "Why I Want to Attend the University of Texas." *Texas Ranger*, 1947.

Texas Exes. *Texas Exes: Precursors—a Salute to the 1956 Black Undergraduates*. Accessed September 9, 2016. https://www.youtube.com/watch?v=nZlLEb5Hs6M.

Texas House Bill 255. 46th Legislative Session. Texas Legislative Reference Library. Accessed July 5, 2017. http://www.lrl.state.tx.us/LASDOCS/46R/HB255 /HB255_46R.pdf#page=649.

Thompson, Rachel. "Whittier Led the Integration of Texas Football Team." *Daily Texan*, May 1, 2012. http://www.dailytexanonline.com/sports/2012/05/01 /whittier-led-the-integration-of-texas-football-team.

Tretter, Eliot M. *Austin Restricted: Progressivism, Zoning, Private Racial Covenants, and the Making of a Segregated City.* Austin: Institute for Urban Policy Research and Analysis, University of Texas at Austin, 2012.

Trillin, Calvin. "Back on the Bus: Remembering the Freedom Riders." *New Yorker*, July 25, 2011. http://www.newyorker.com/magazine/2011/07/25/back-on-the-bus.

Weddell, Wray. "Library's Ban on Negroes Hits." *Austin American-Statesman*, September 21, 1951, Part A.

ABOUT THE EDITORS

■ **GREGORY J. VINCENT**

Dr. Gregory J. Vincent is currently the 16th president of Hobart and William Smith Colleges in Geneva, New York. He previously served as the University of Texas at Austin vice president for diversity and community engagement from 2006–17. Vincent came to UT Austin in 2005 as vice provost for inclusion and cross-cultural effectiveness. While at UT Austin, he held the W.K. Kellogg Professorship for Community College Leadership and was professor of law. He earned his law degree from the Ohio State University Moritz College of Law and doctorate from the University of Pennsylvania.

Under Vincent's tenure, the UT Division of Diversity and Community Engagement grew to encompass more than 50 units and projects, including the exemplary rated UT Elementary School, the university's Office for Inclusion and Equity, a new Community Engagement Center, the University Interscholastic League, the Hogg Foundation for Mental Health, and a number of successful initiatives that work to increase the number of first-generation college students and students from underrepresented populations in the higher education.

■ **VIRGINIA A. CUMBERBATCH**

Virginia Cumberbatch serves as director of the Community Engagement Center (CEC), a part of the University of Texas at Austin (UT) Division of Diversity and Community Engagement (DDCE). Cumberbatch has used her years of academic and professional experience to facilitate conversations about diversity, inclusion and equity throughout the Austin area. In her current capacity, Virginia ensures that the center continues to develop new and sustain mutually beneficial partnerships between the University of Texas and diverse communities, improving systems to be more accessible and equitable for historically underscrved communities. She received her bachelor's degree in history at Williams College and her master's degree in Public Affairs at the Lyndon B. Johnson School of Public Affairs at UT. In 2016, she was the recipient of the Austin Anti-Defamation League's Social Justice Award.

■ LESLIE ASHER BLAIR

Leslie Blair is executive director of communications for the Division of Diversity and Community Engagement at the University of Texas at Austin. She has worked in the Division since 2008, helping to establish the brand and communication strategies for the division. Previously Blair worked as a communications associate and project director at the Southwest Educational Development Laboratory and as a newspaper reporter in Las Cruces, NM. She began her career at the Texas State Historical Association and Center for Studies in Texas History at UT Austin soon after graduating from college. Blair holds a bachelor's degree in Journalism from Texas State University and a master's degree in English from New Mexico State University. She has edited five books on leadership and change in schools and has received several awards from the Association of Educational Publishers.

INDEX

Page numbers in italic indicate photographs.